Inside the Burlesque Boudoir
An Intimate Study In Photography

"The new wave of burlesque during the 00s created more opportunities to stage cabaret. A new audience and the growing attraction of burlesque created a flourishing scene, with many artists producing shows and acts with original and decadent material. It was new, fresh and exciting."

Empress Stah

"Debby's photos take us beyond the level of intimacy captured backstage and into a further sense of the performer's boudoir. For me, it was important to work with a female photographer. Debby understands the differences between a woman's performative space and her private domestic one."

Stella Starr

Documentary photographer Debby Besford spent the years between 2005-7 researching and photographing complex stories around the representation of the contemporary female, with emphasis on the Burlesque stage performer.

This project celebrates the idea of play between the photographer and the performer's private space. The images juxtapose fantasy and reality, combining a sense of empowerment and the mystique of each woman's identity and her private space. The domestic interiors are in themselves a theatre, where the lives of the performers take on a different persona.

For many, the 21st century New Burlesque Revival is seen as a response to women's desires to explore and enjoy their identity and challenge societal expectations, a movement in celebrating femininity through a staged persona. Burlesque is a powerful art form where the performer has the freedom to push artistic boundaries, entertain, inspire and provoke a captive audience.

This body of work evolved from a deep-rooted curiosity around female sexuality and the traditional aspects we assume regarding female identity within western society. Modern burlesque includes performers from different backgrounds, genders, sexualities, all shapes, sizes, encouraging a strong camaraderie, collaboration and community. There is a wonderful array of storytelling in the performances blending comedy, politics, activism, poetry, dance, to trapeze acts and fire eating. This diversity of styles, costumes and influences, including vaudeville to punk rock and drag, are dazzling, saucy and humorous.

Collaborating with these women was a journey of immense trust and respect. Debby wasn't seeking to deconstruct the female performer stereotype or their bedrooms, but instead explore and celebrate how these women embrace and cherish their performer identities, joyfully sharing the fantasies linked to public representation of their unique acts.

These images offer subtle visual clues around the performer's private worlds, stimulating our imagination. We are encouraged to question our interpretation of the female performer and to question her 'separate' identity.

For these women, the performance of acting out a character and demonstrating their creativity is both liberating and empowering.

In this collection we invite you to observe the personal intimate space of each performer's boudoir, and to notice and appreciate the finer details within the images that might tell you more about the personality behind the public character.

For Debby, to be invited into these fascinating women's lives in such an intimate, trusting way was a huge privilege and gave her insight and clarity, through the lens of the female gaze, to discover her own empowerment, creativity and feminine identity.

Debby Besford

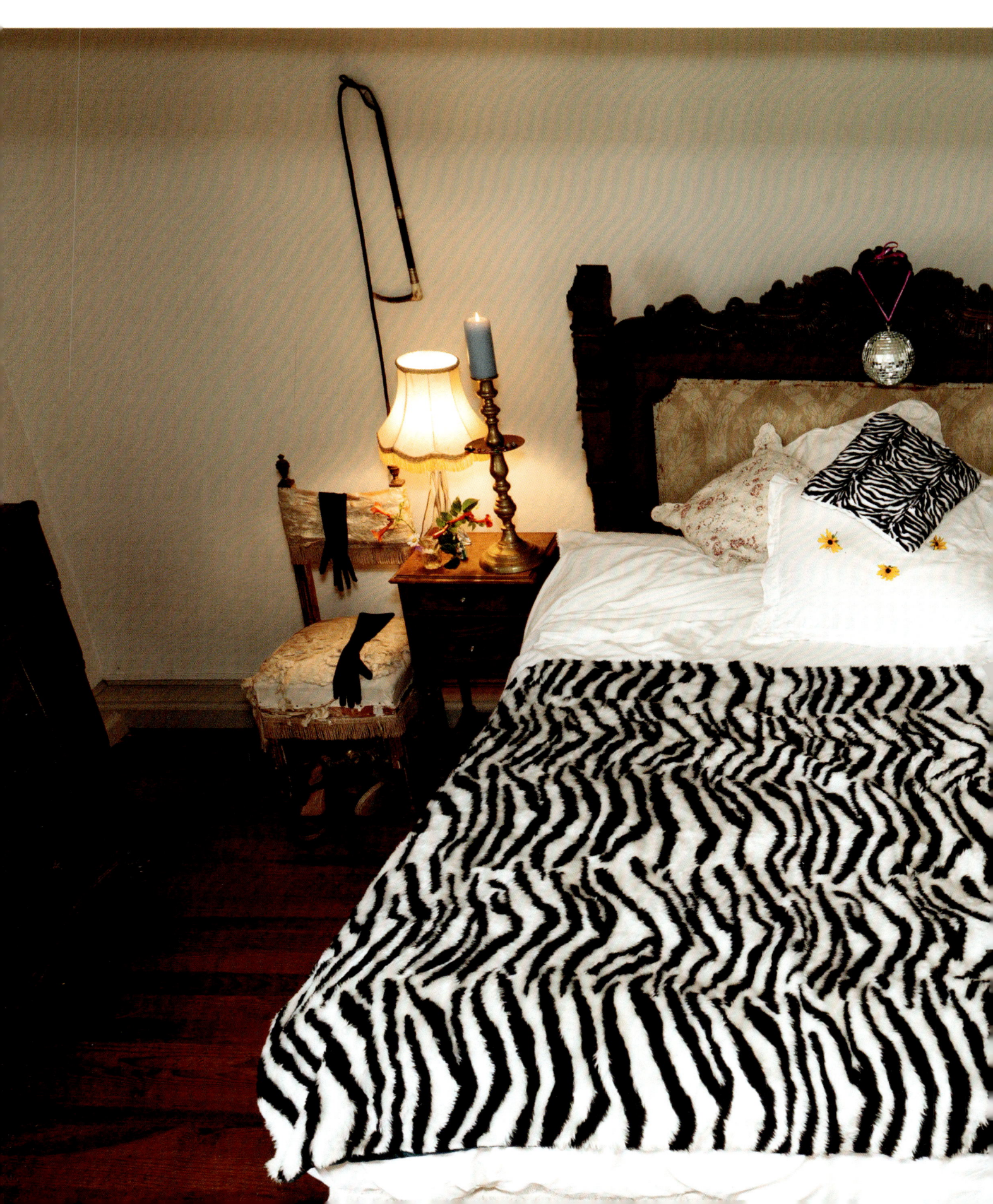

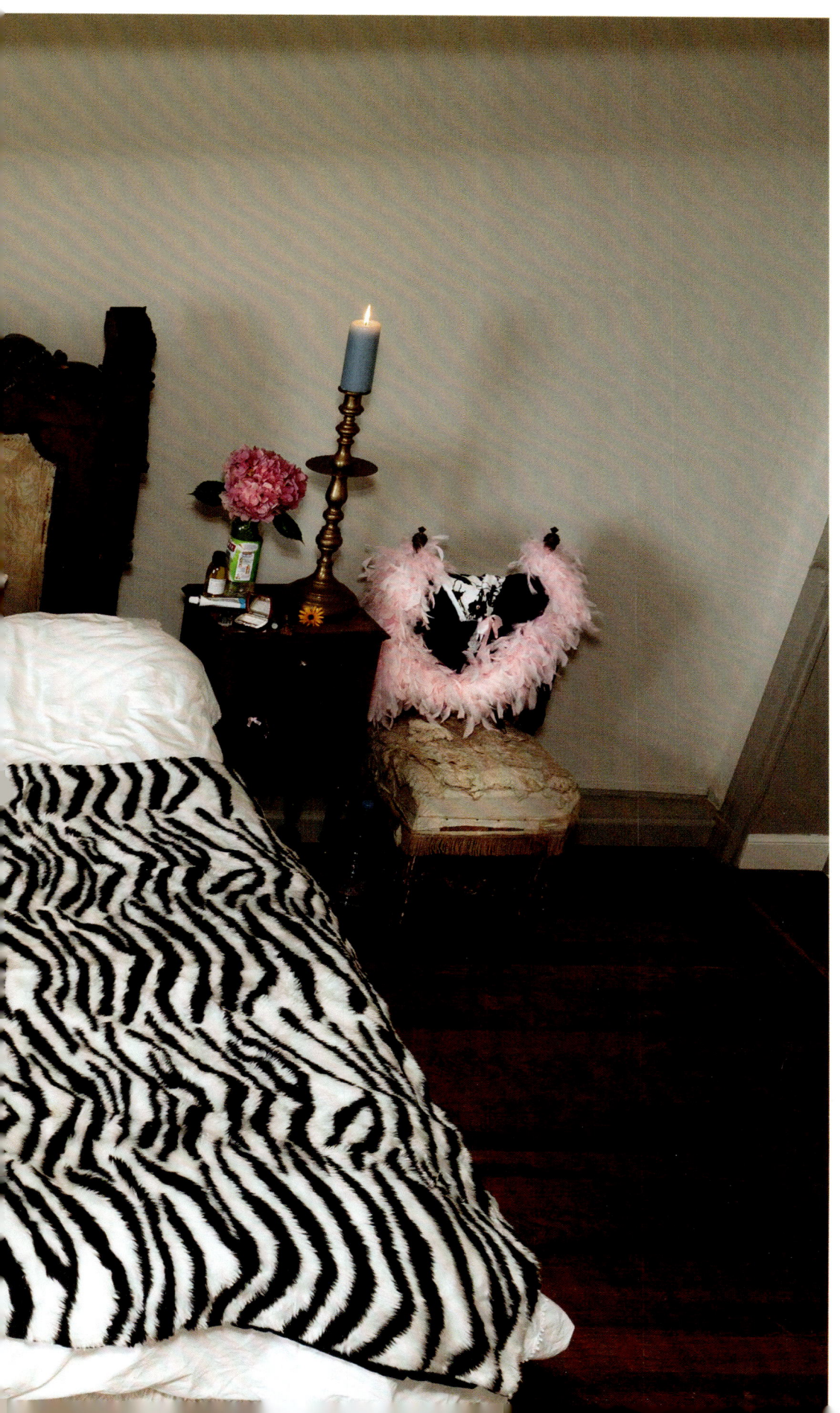

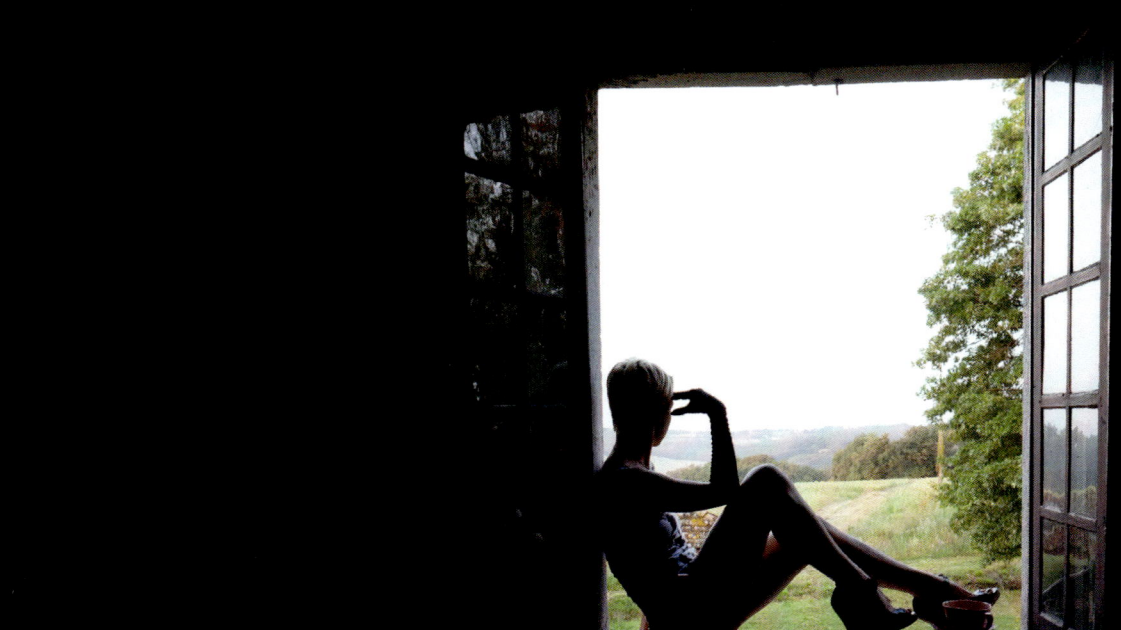

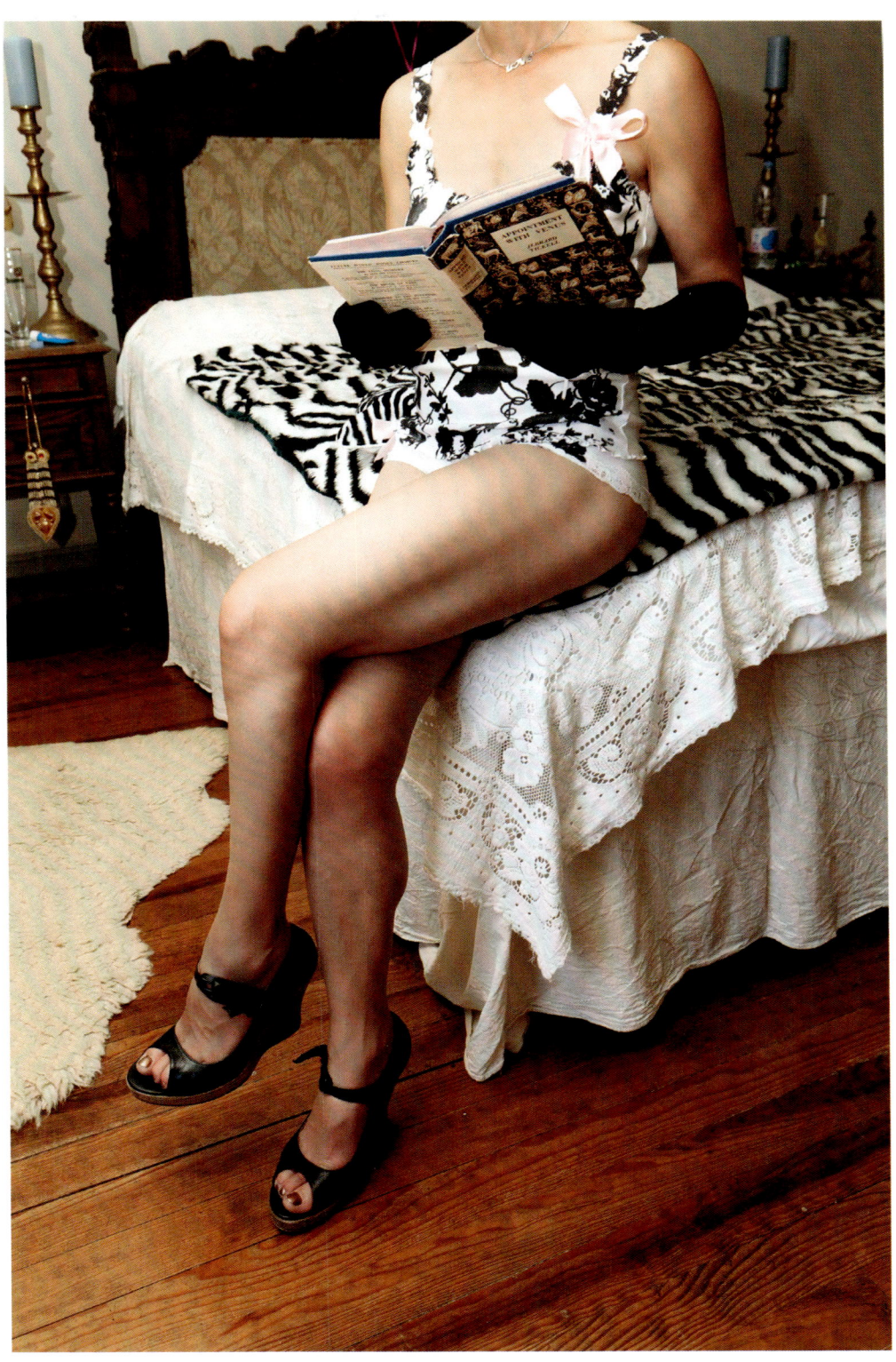

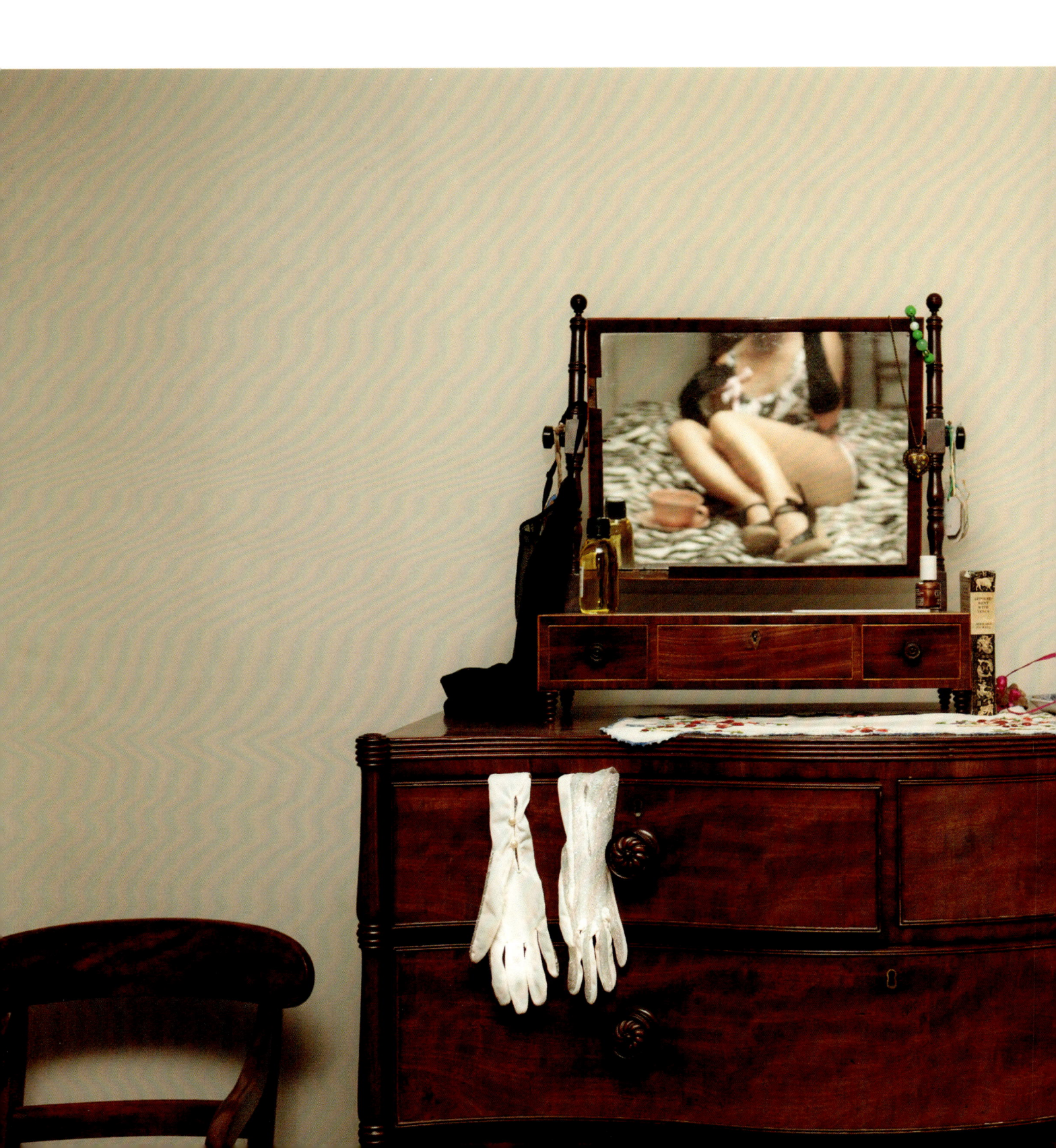

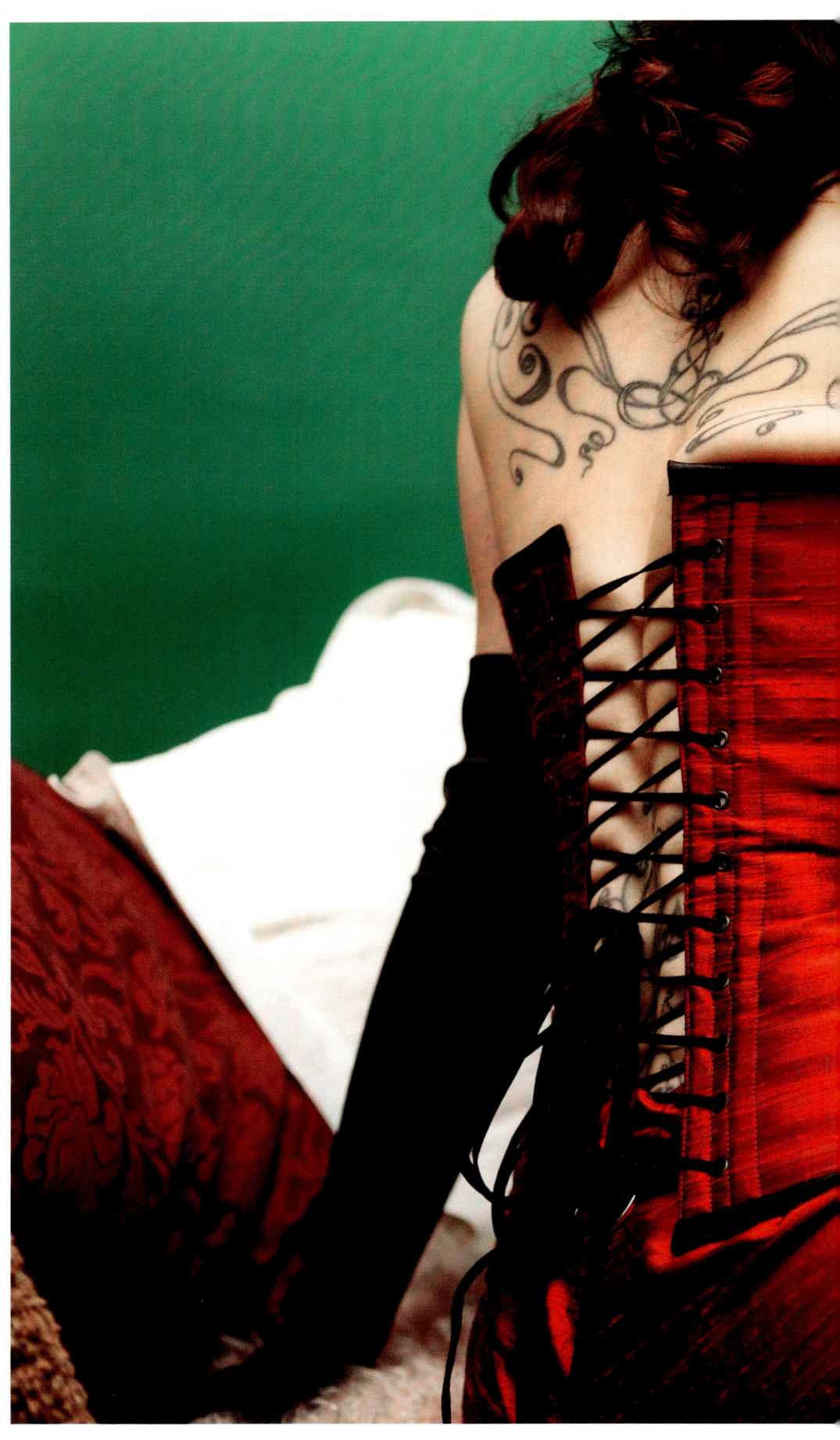

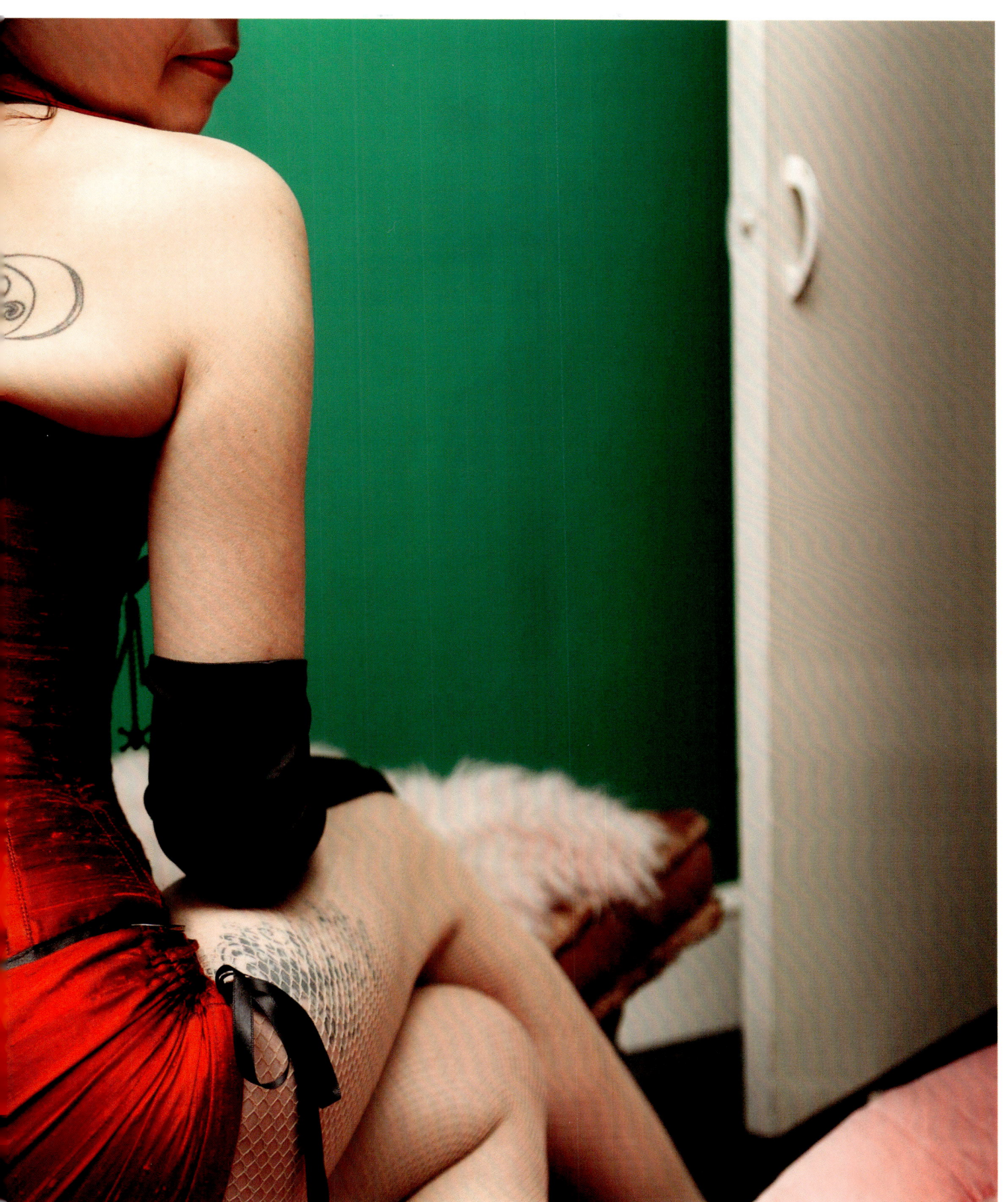

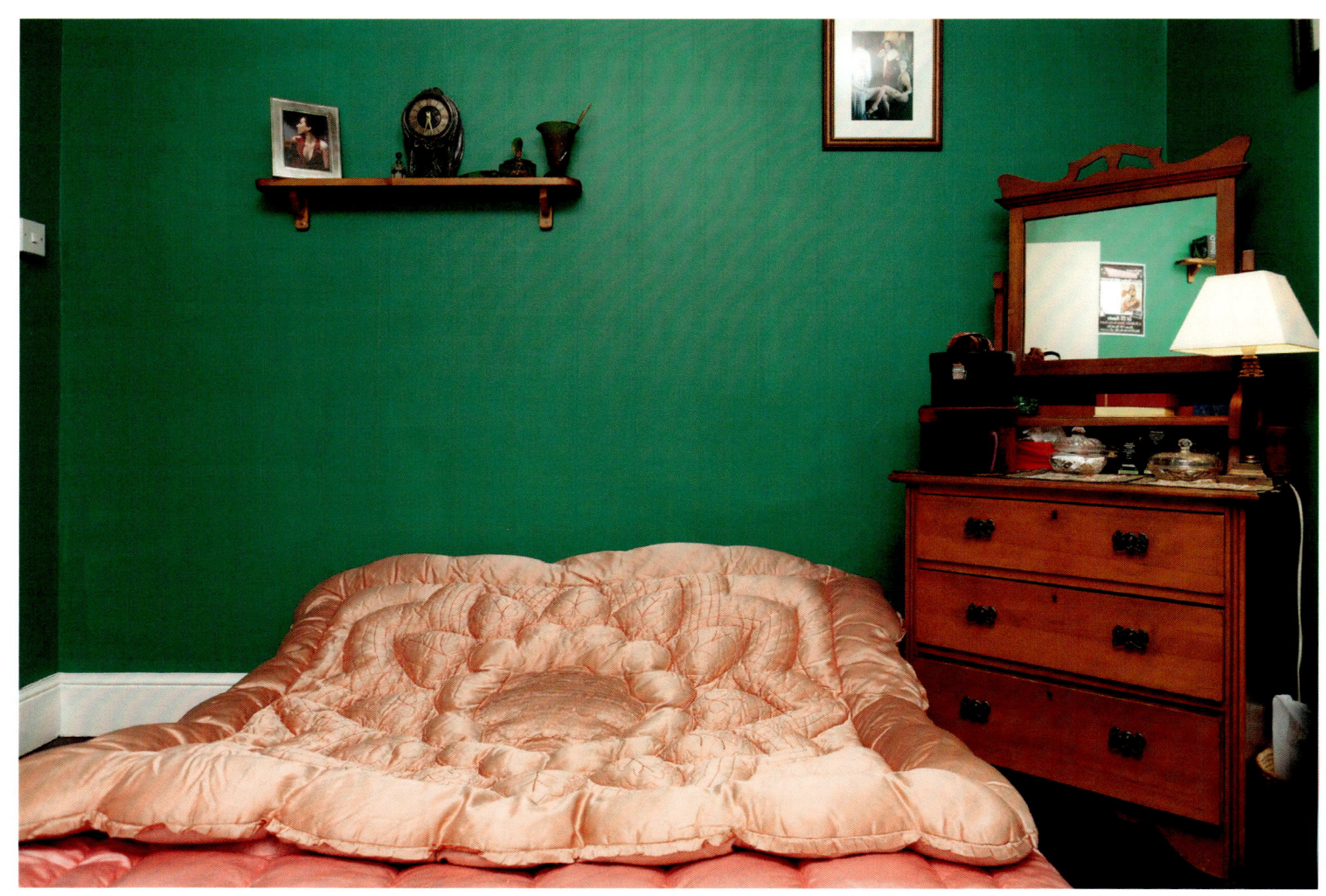

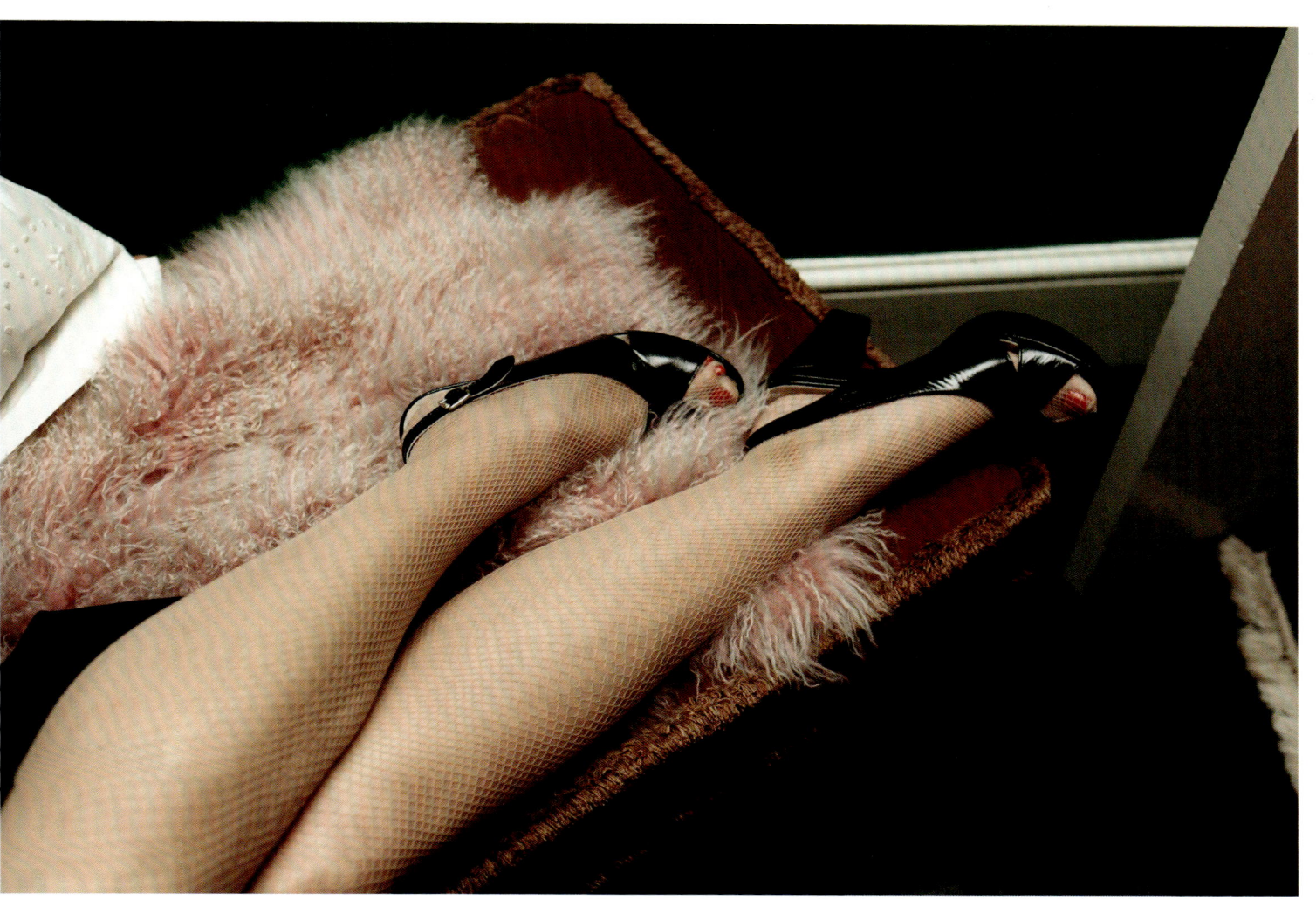

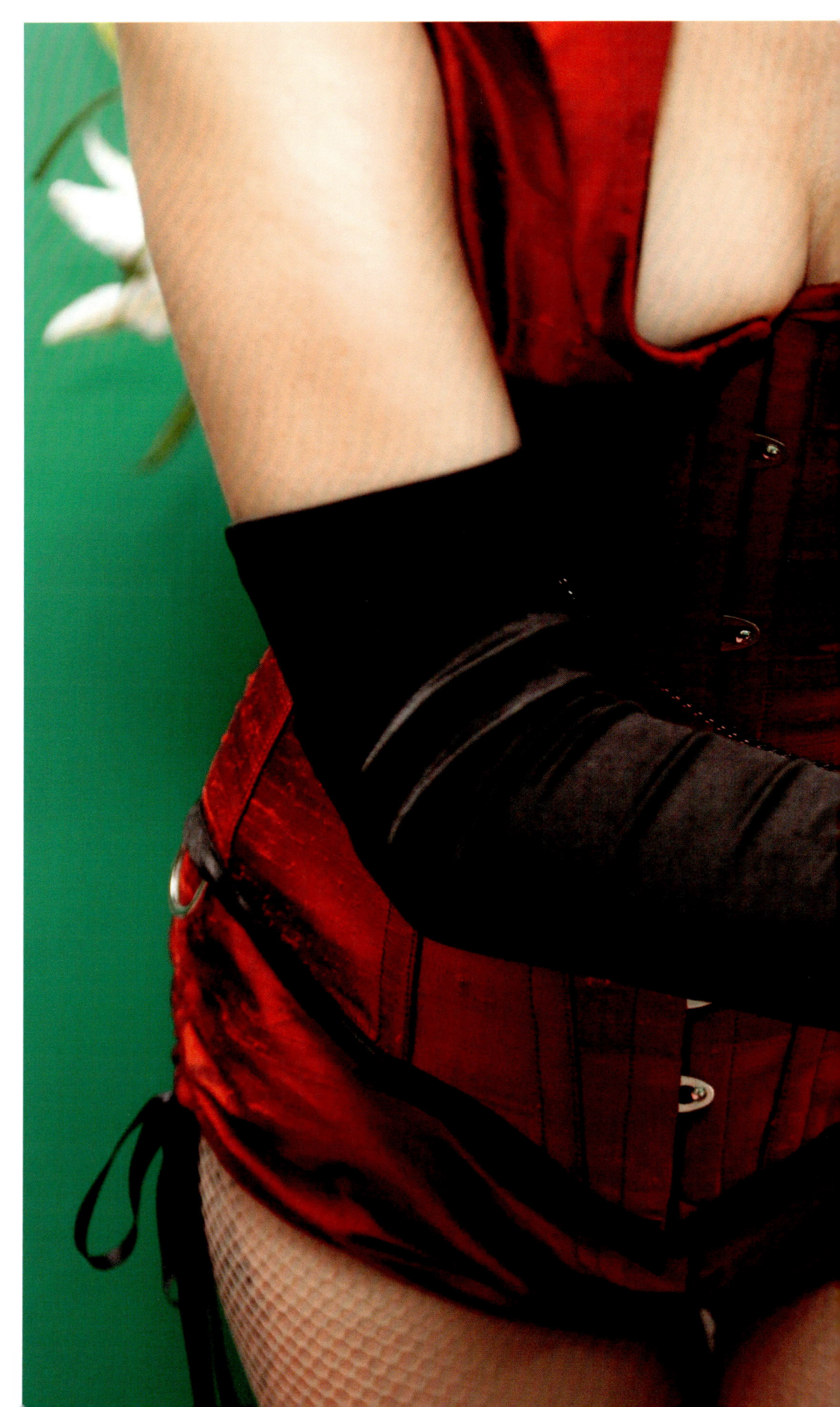

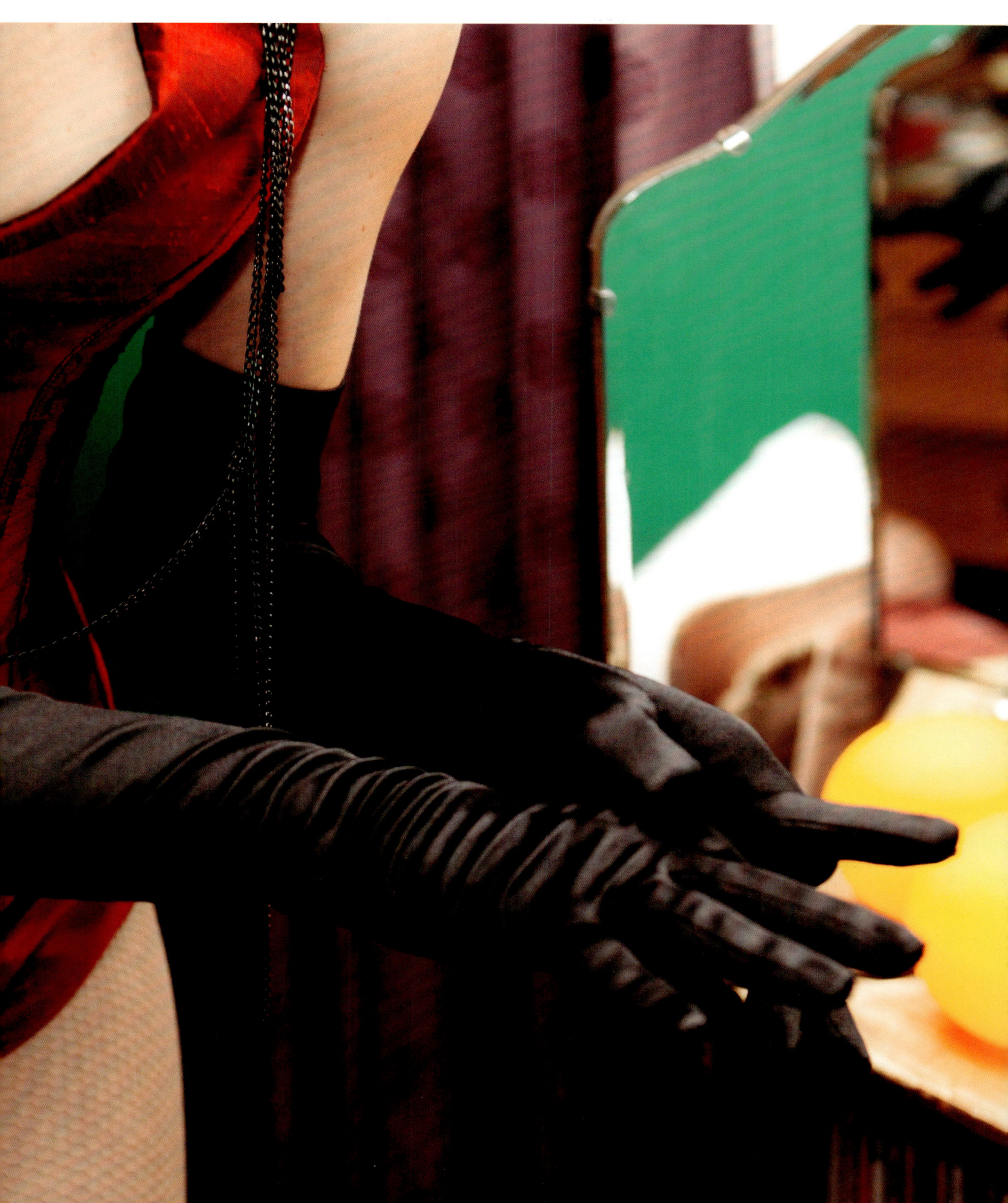

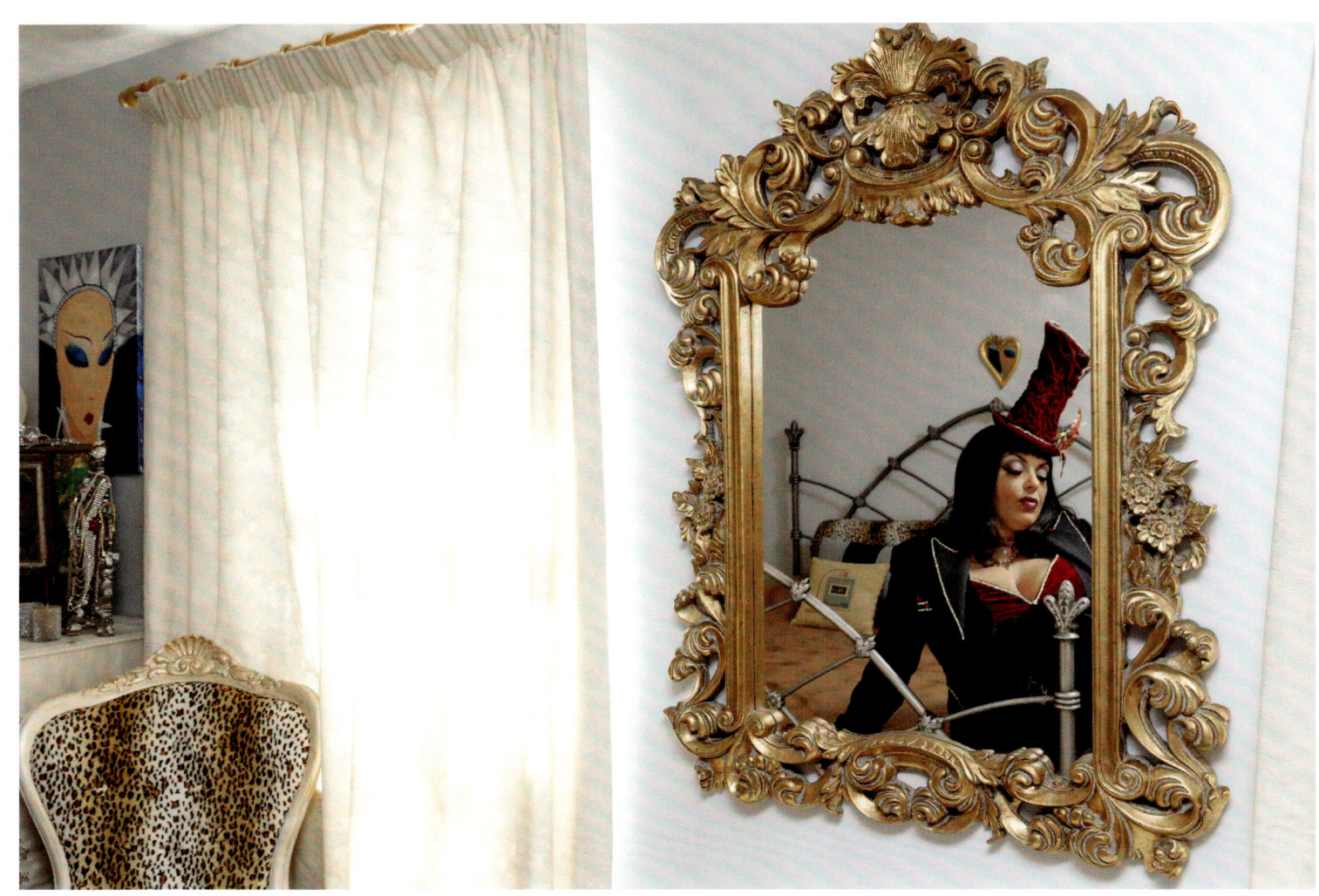

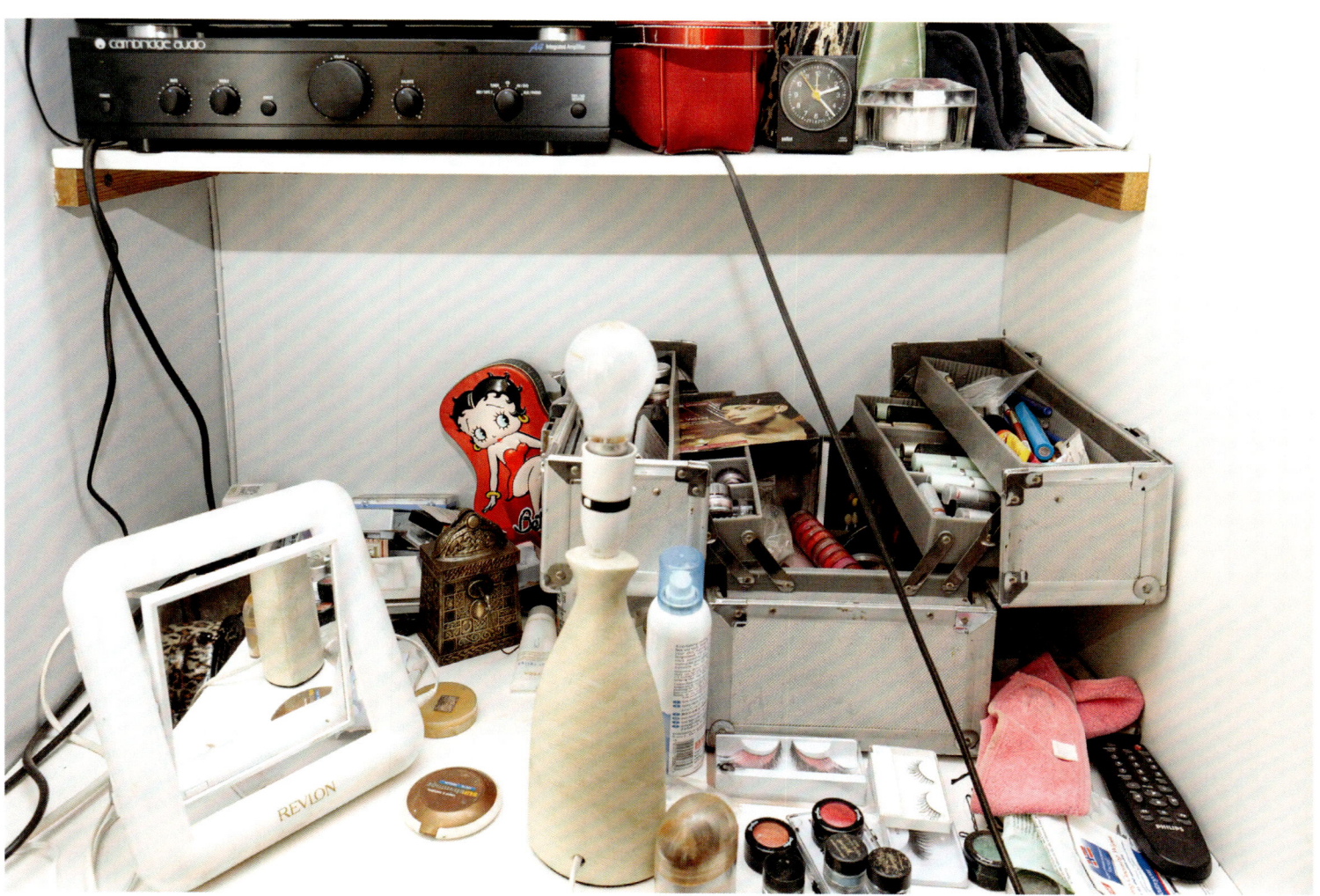

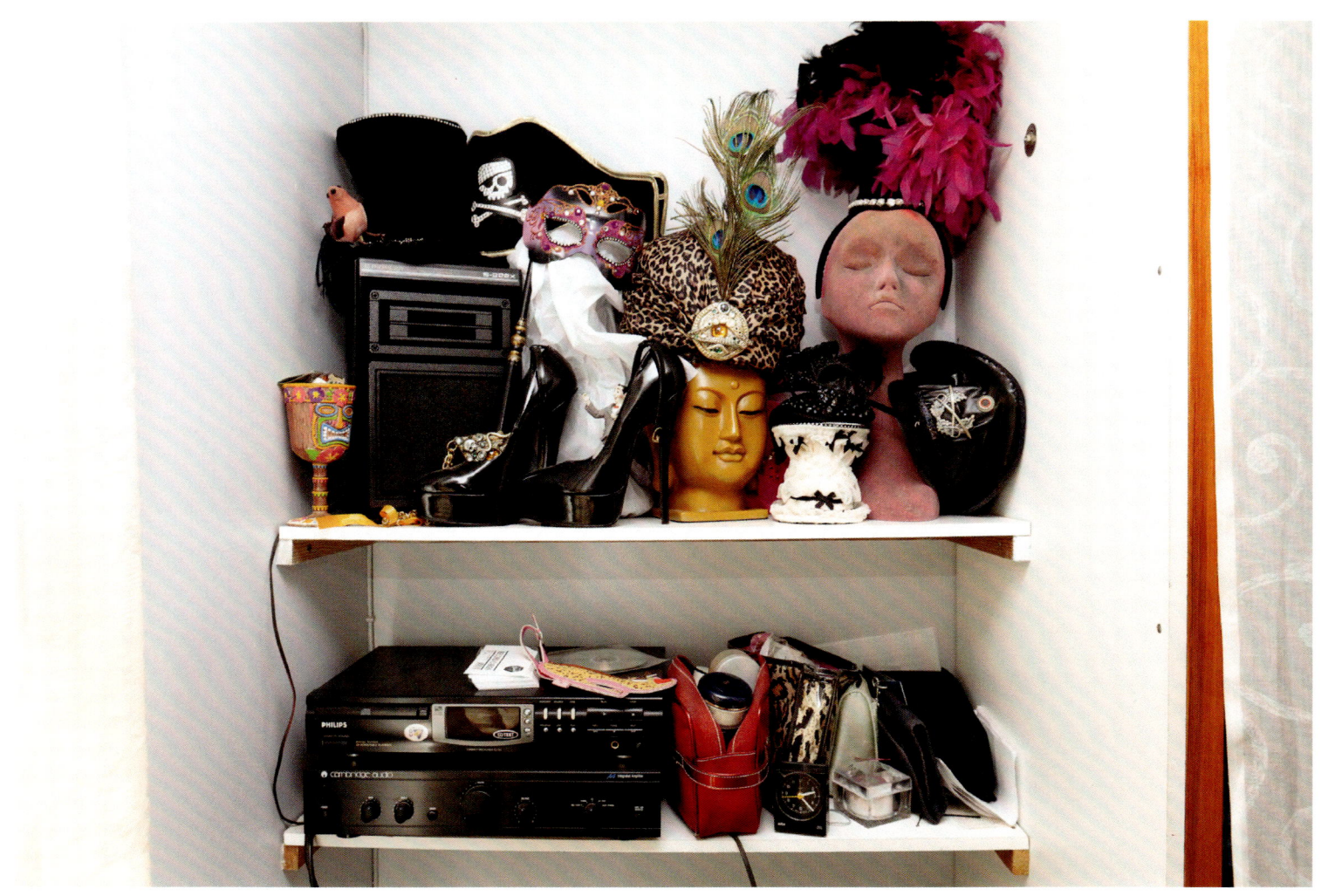

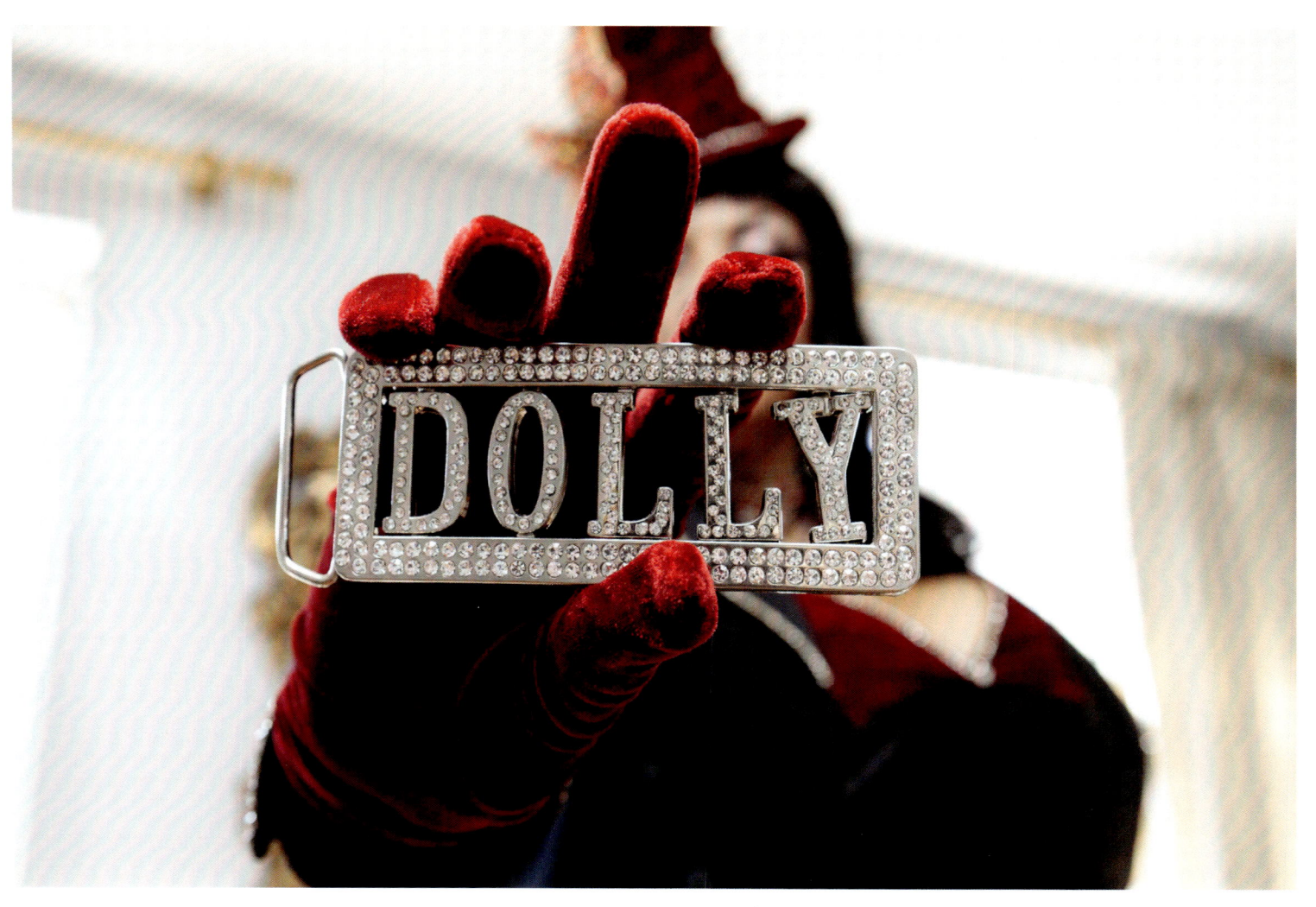

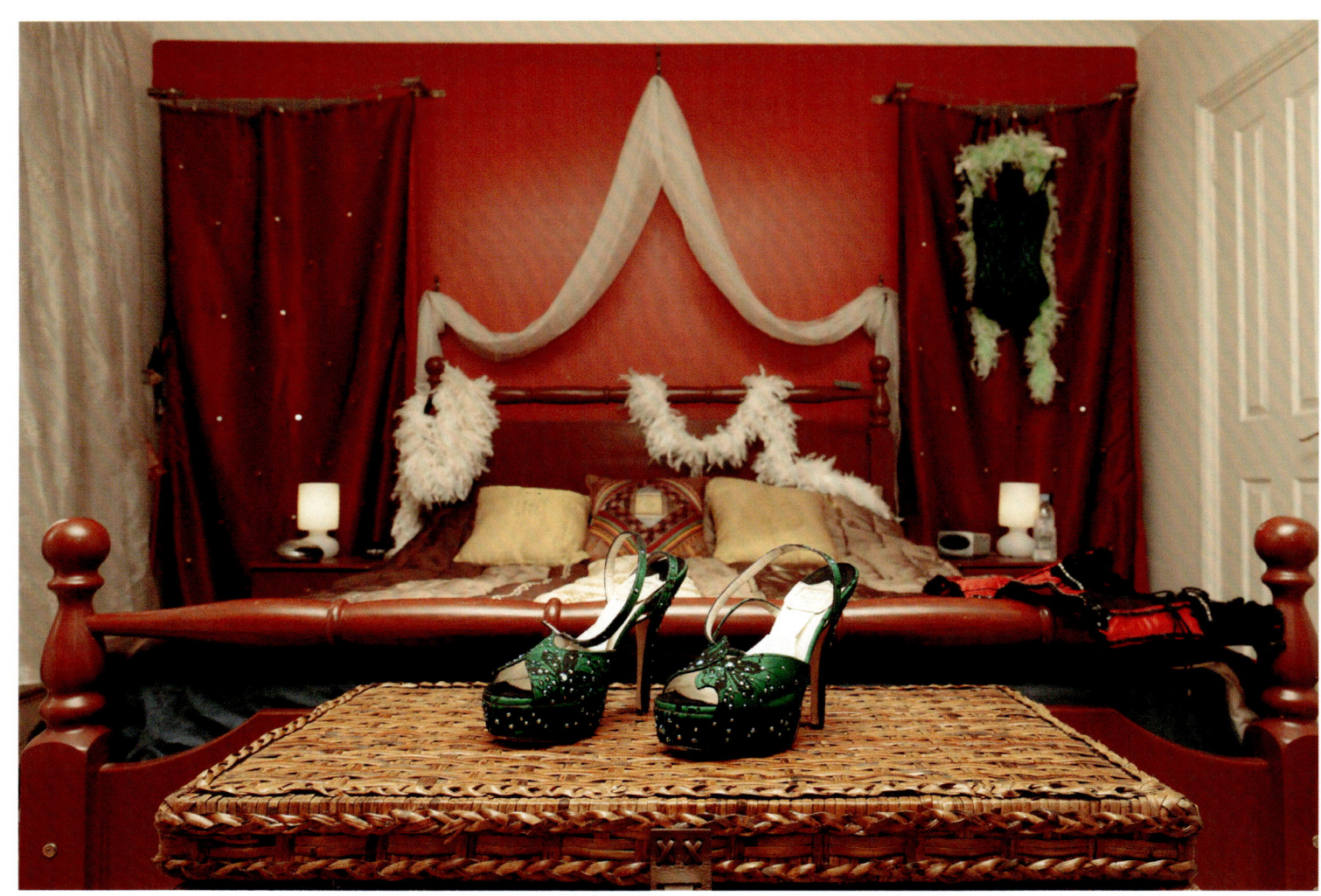

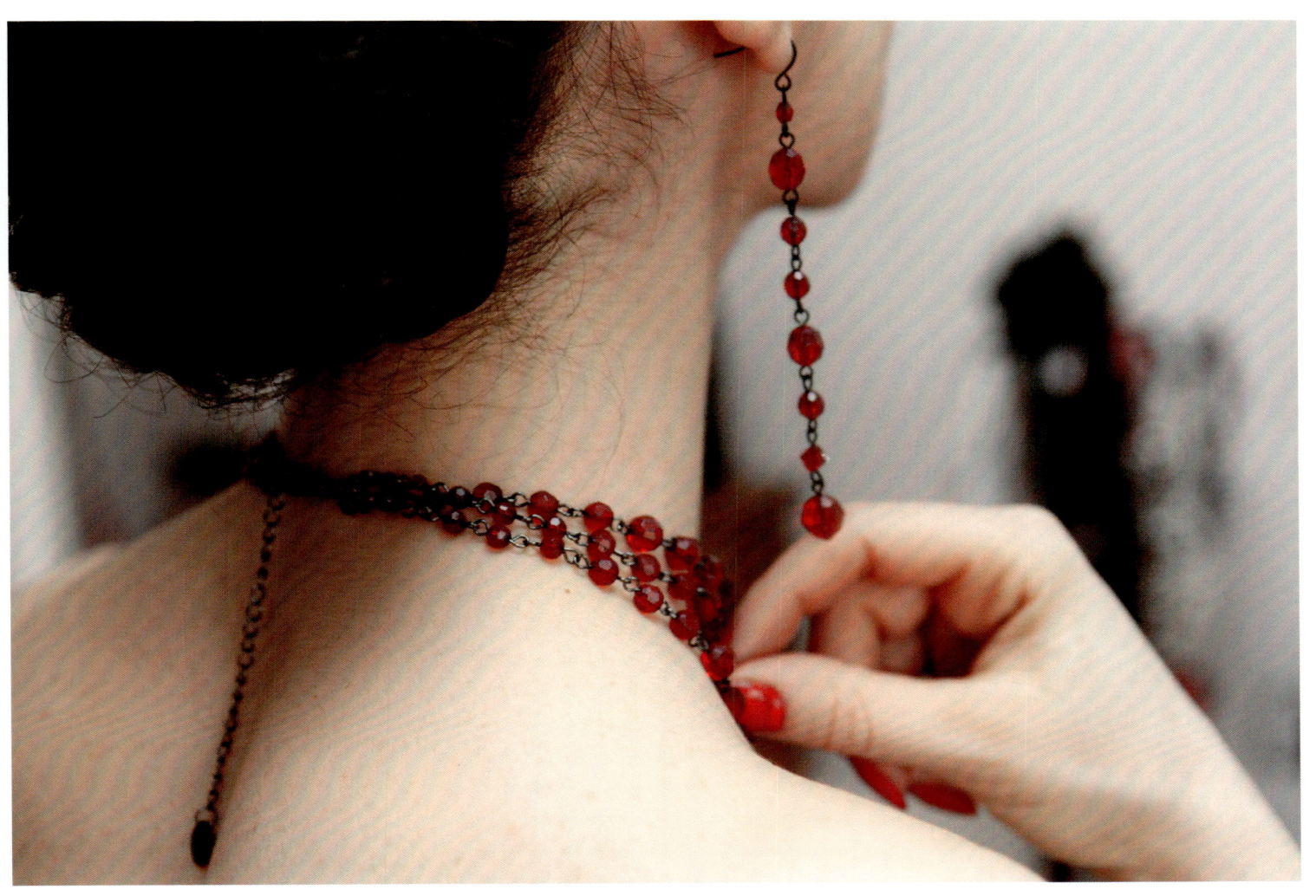

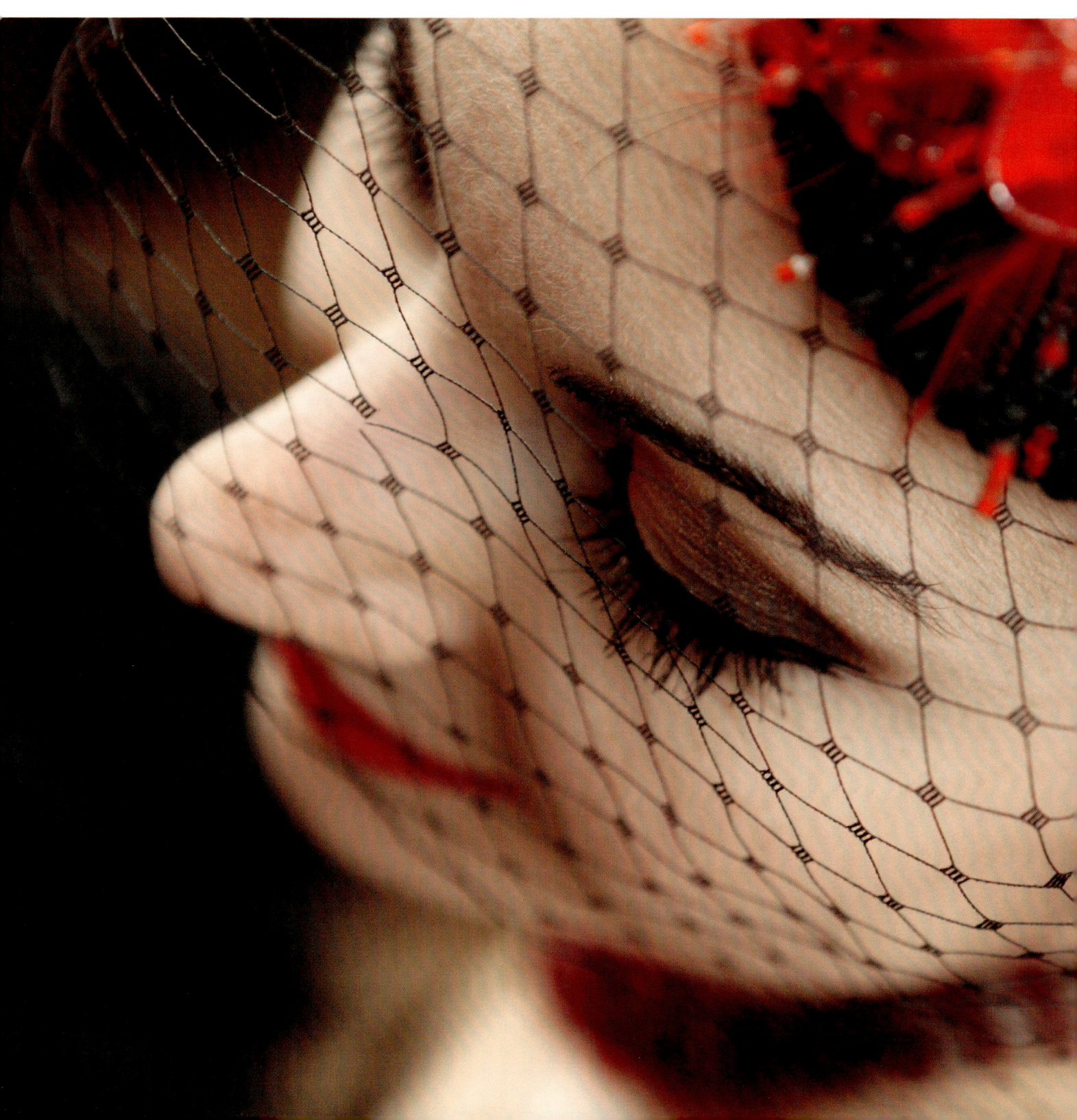

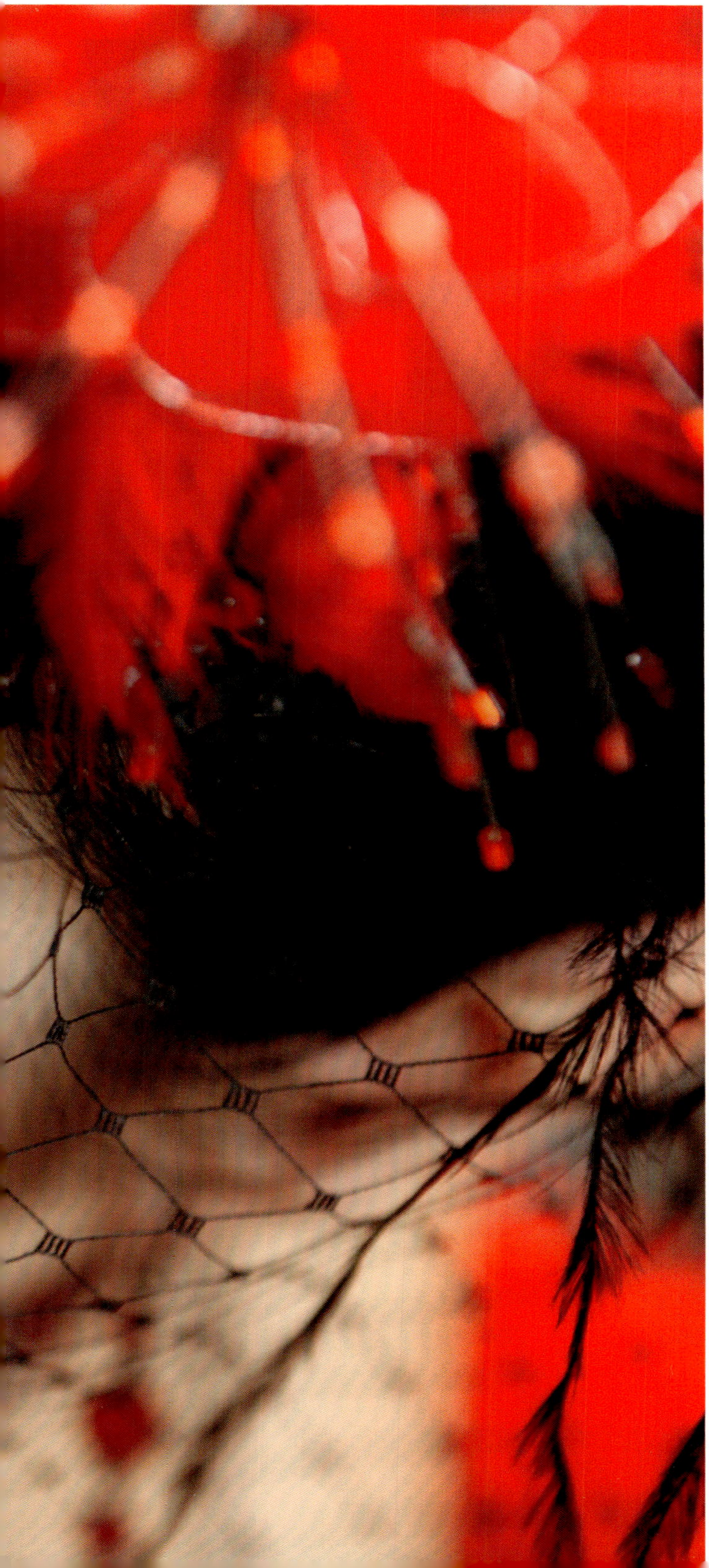

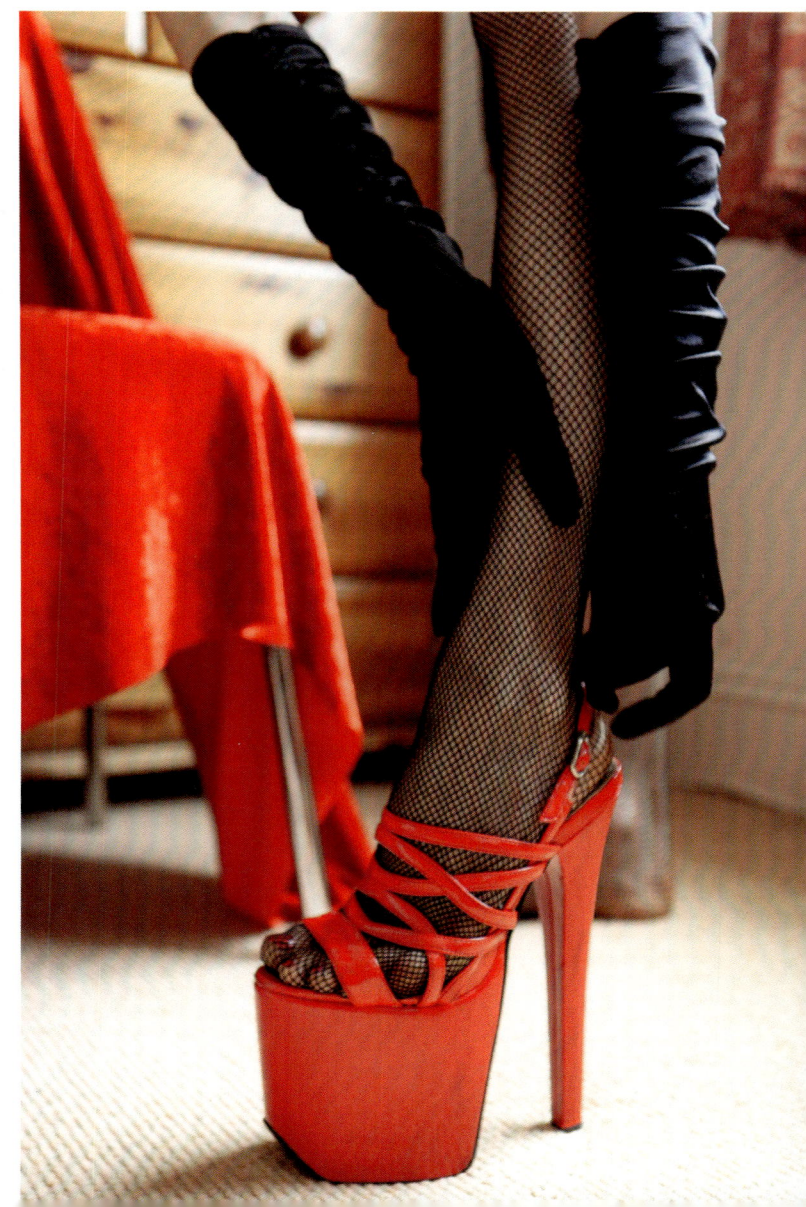

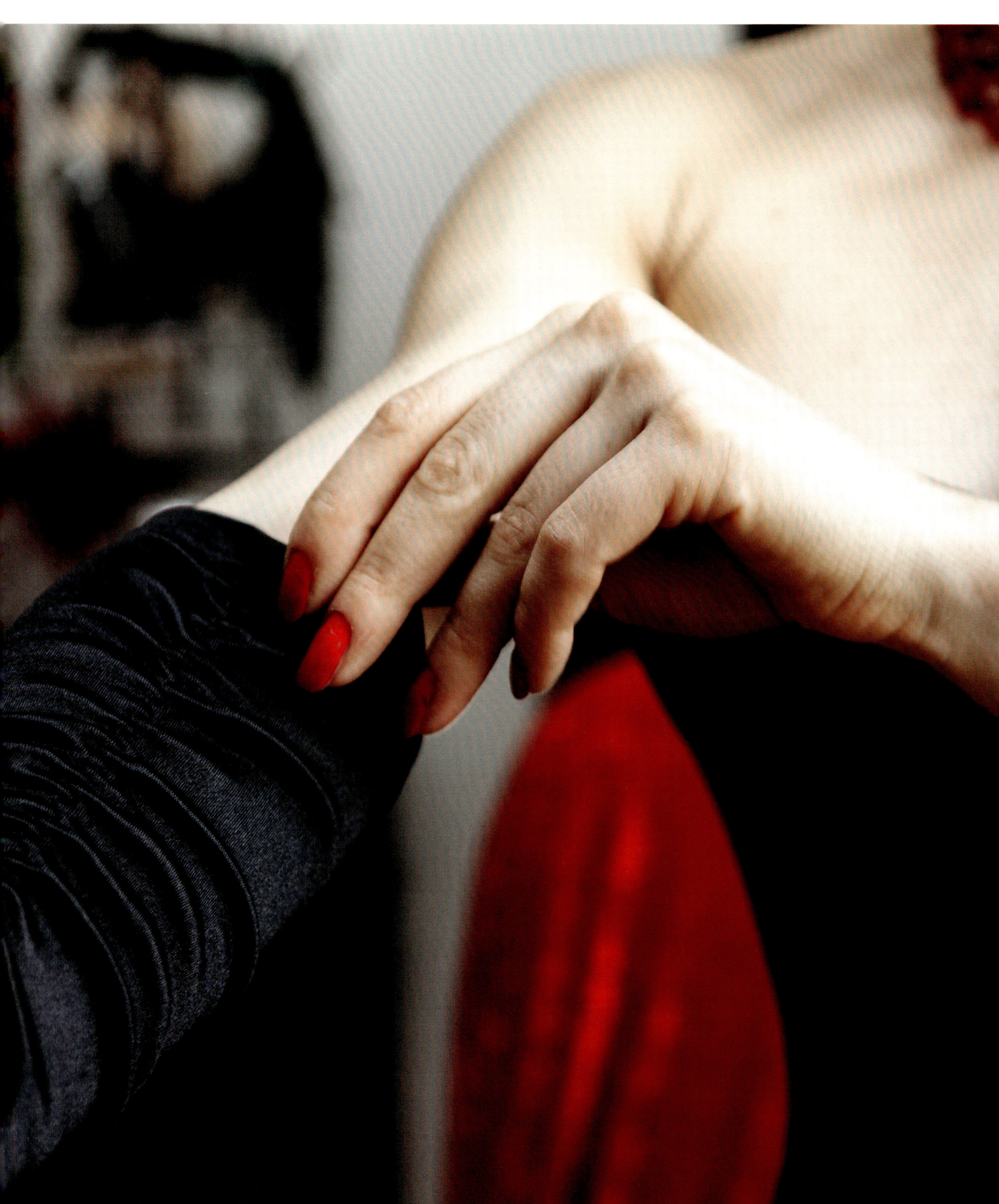

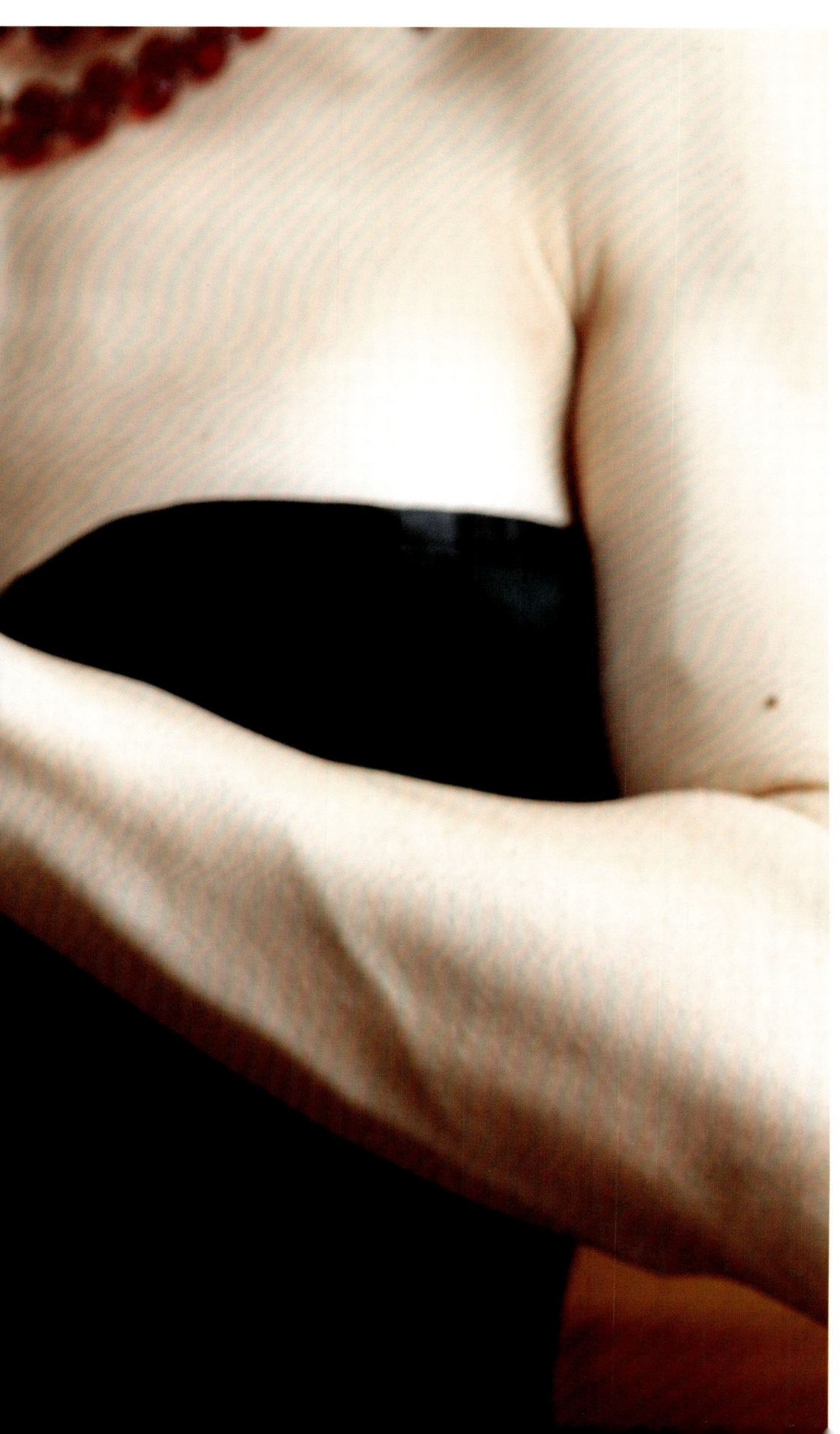

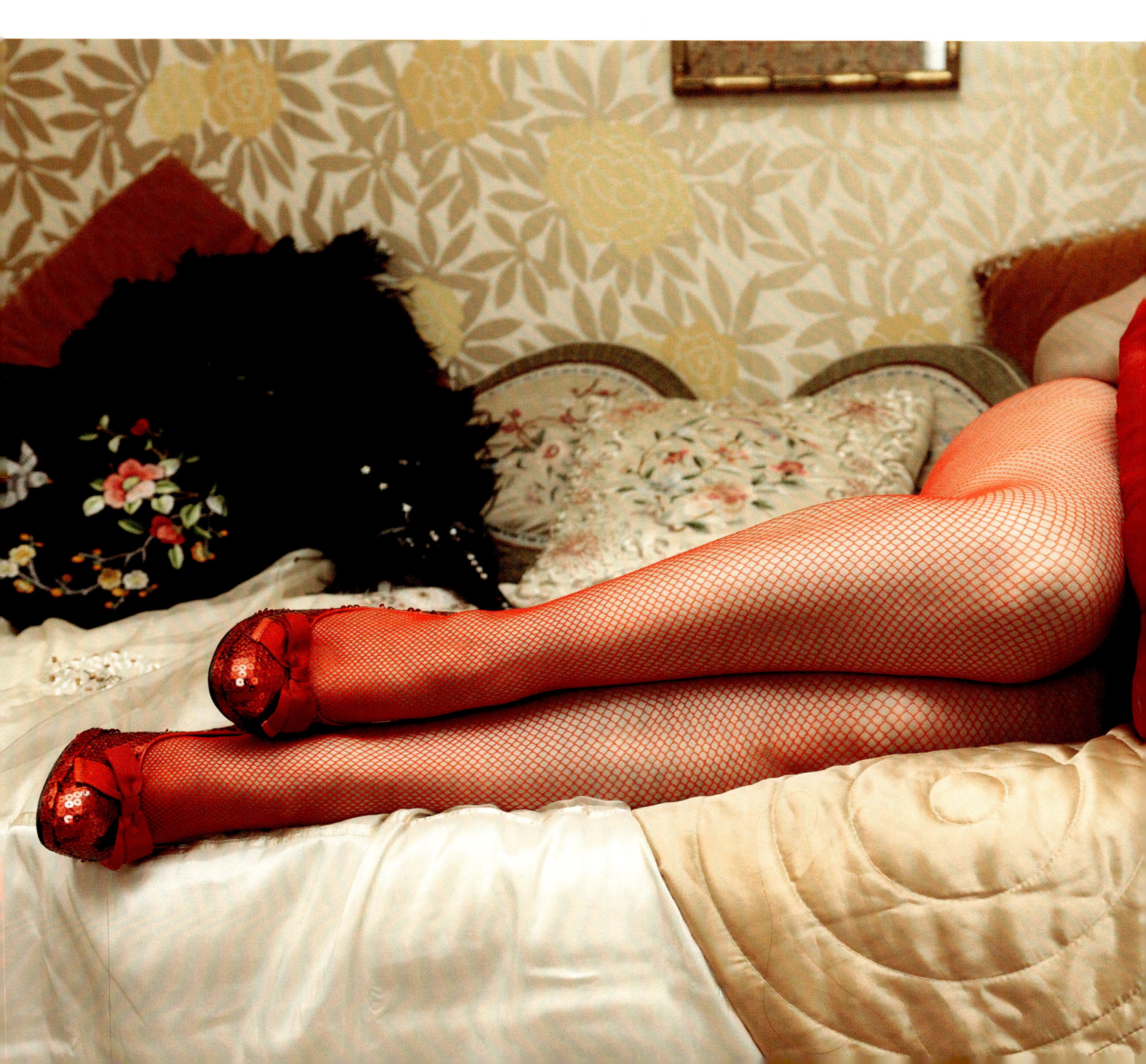

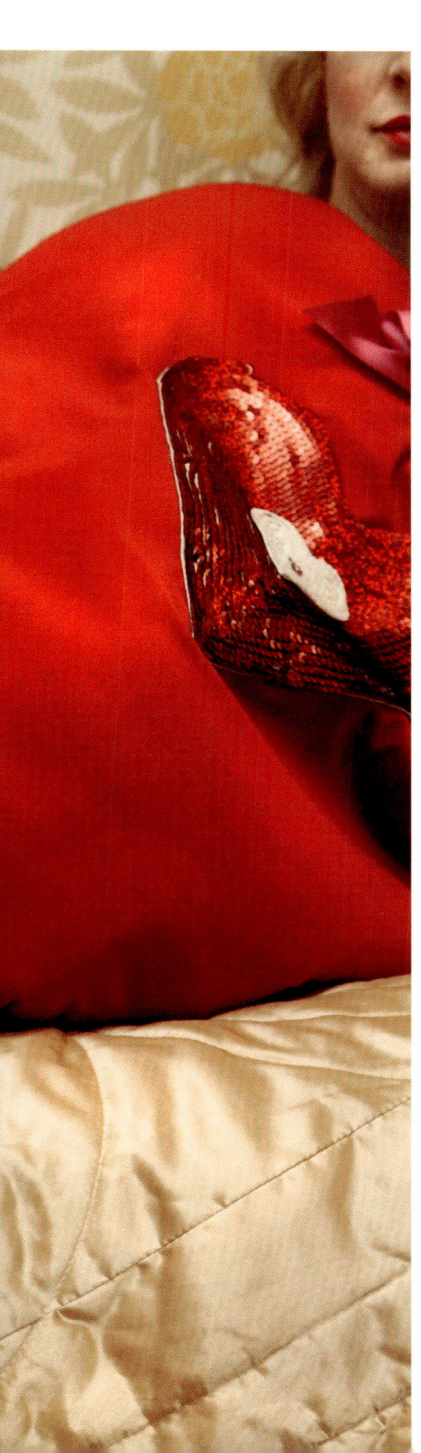

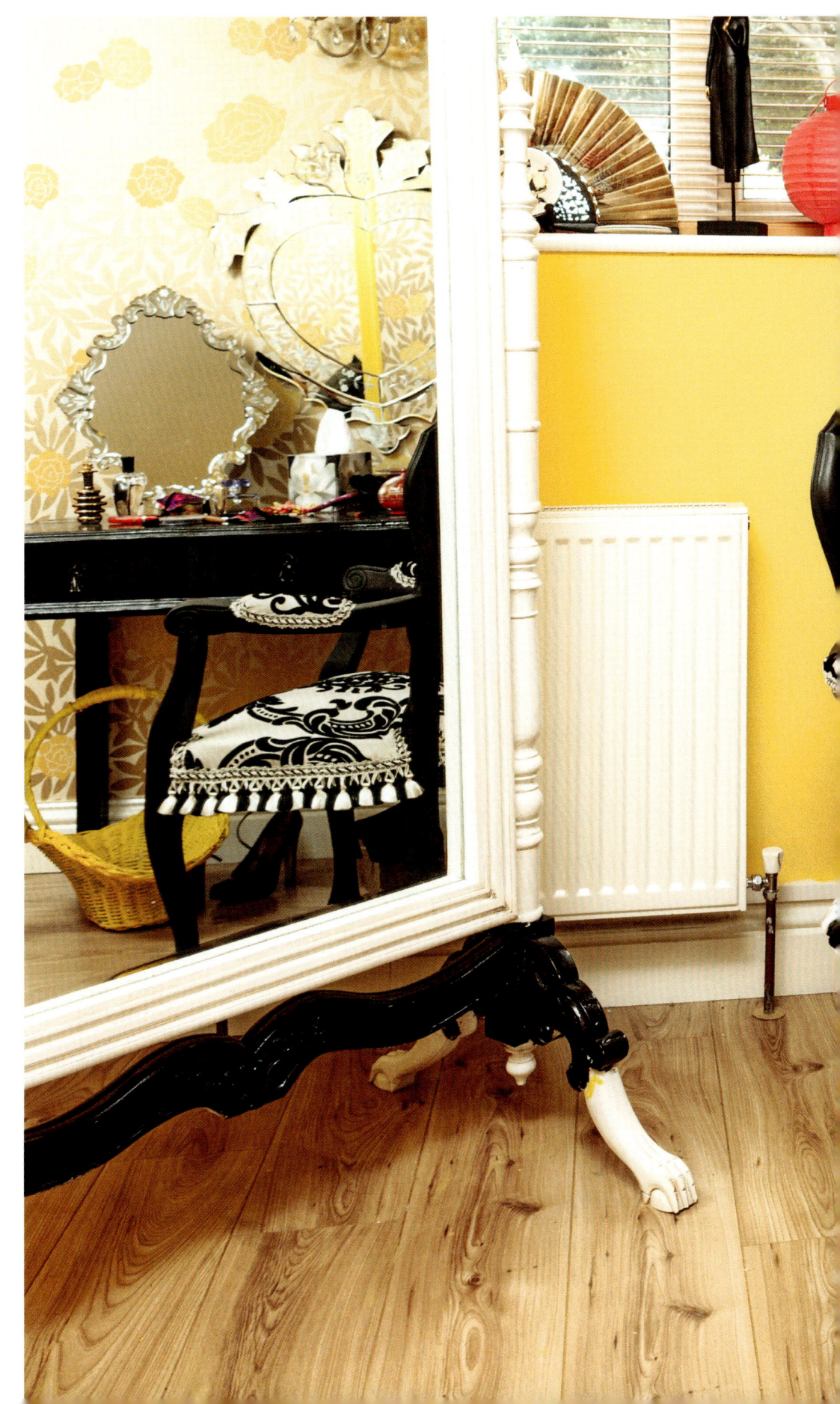

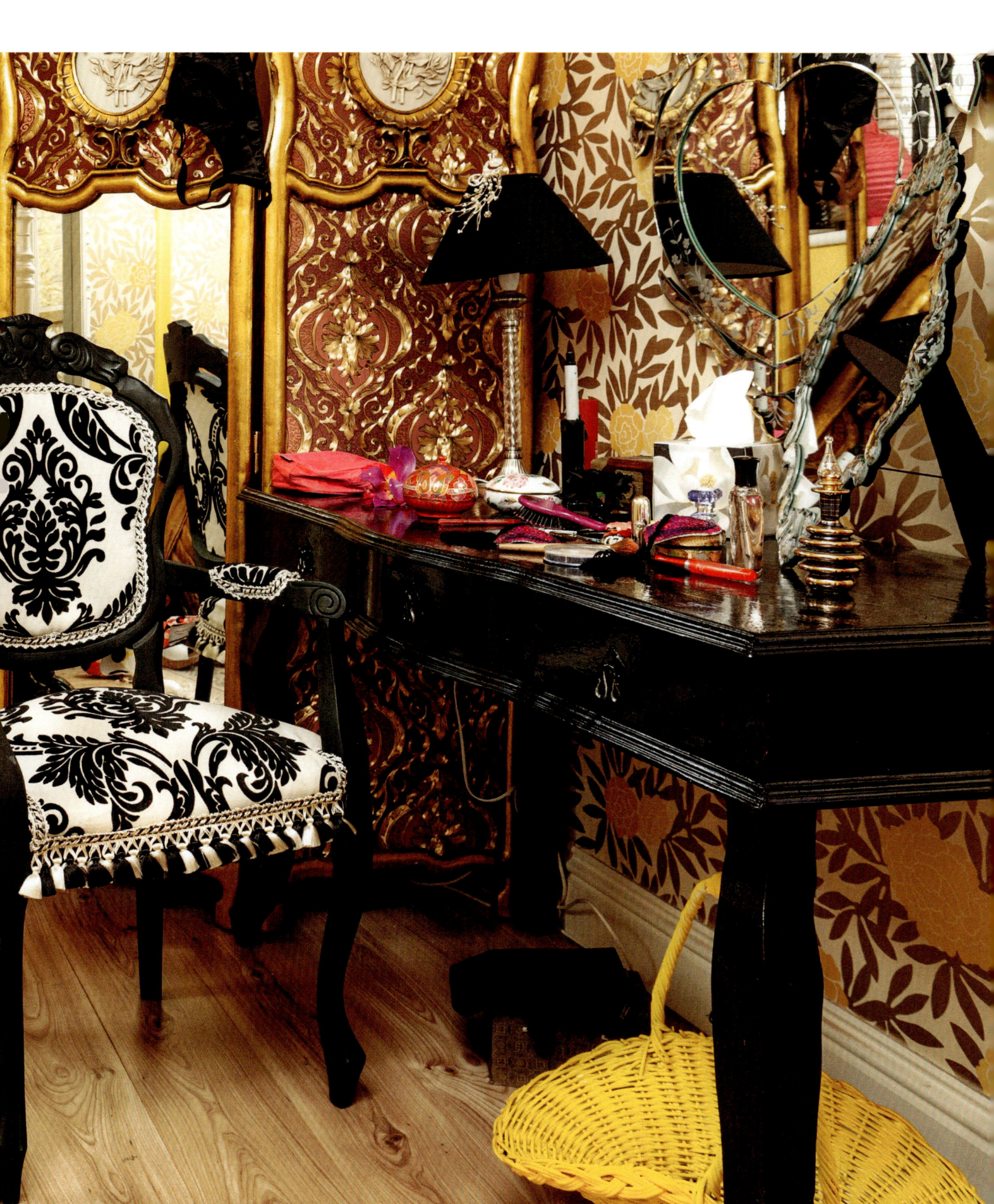

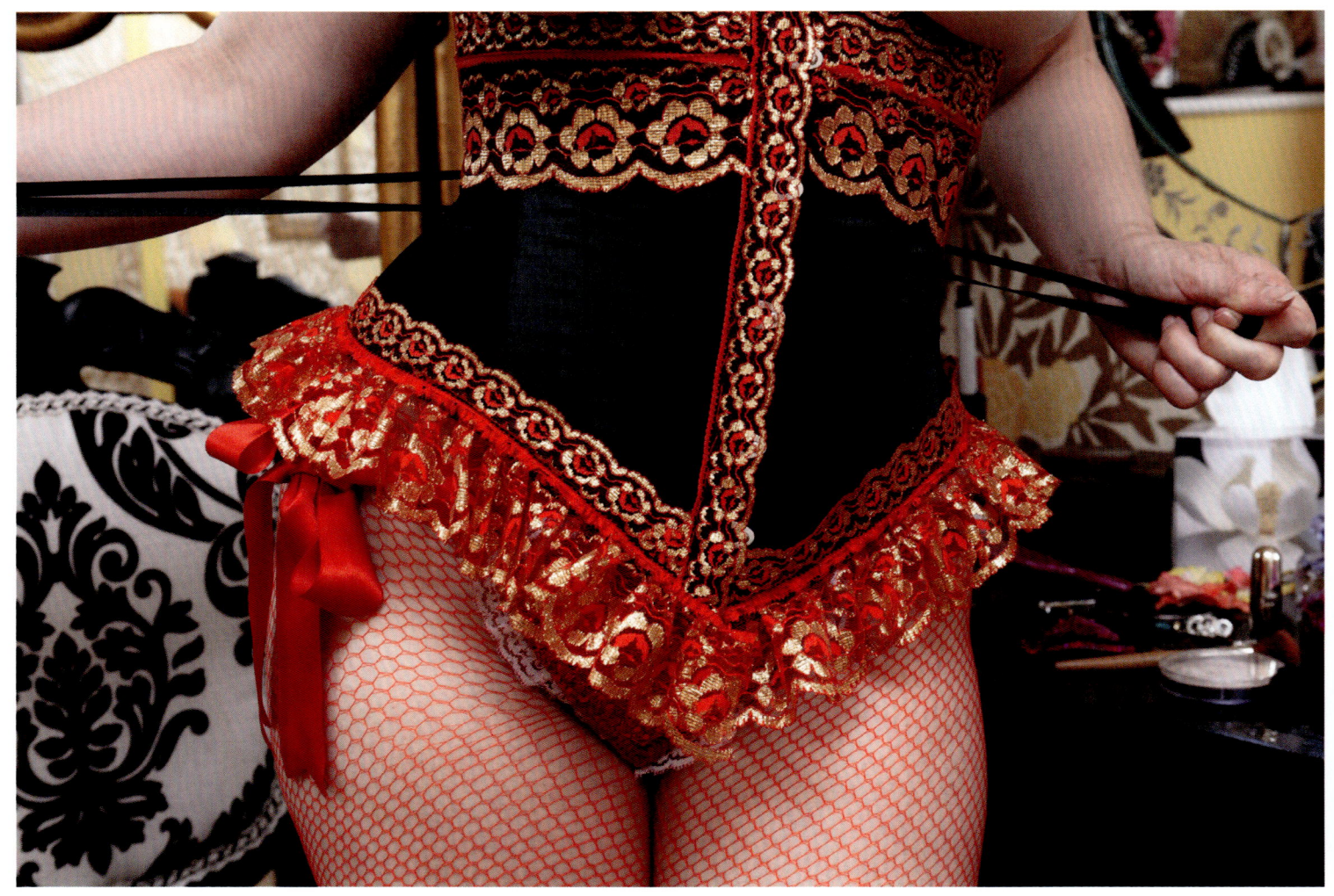

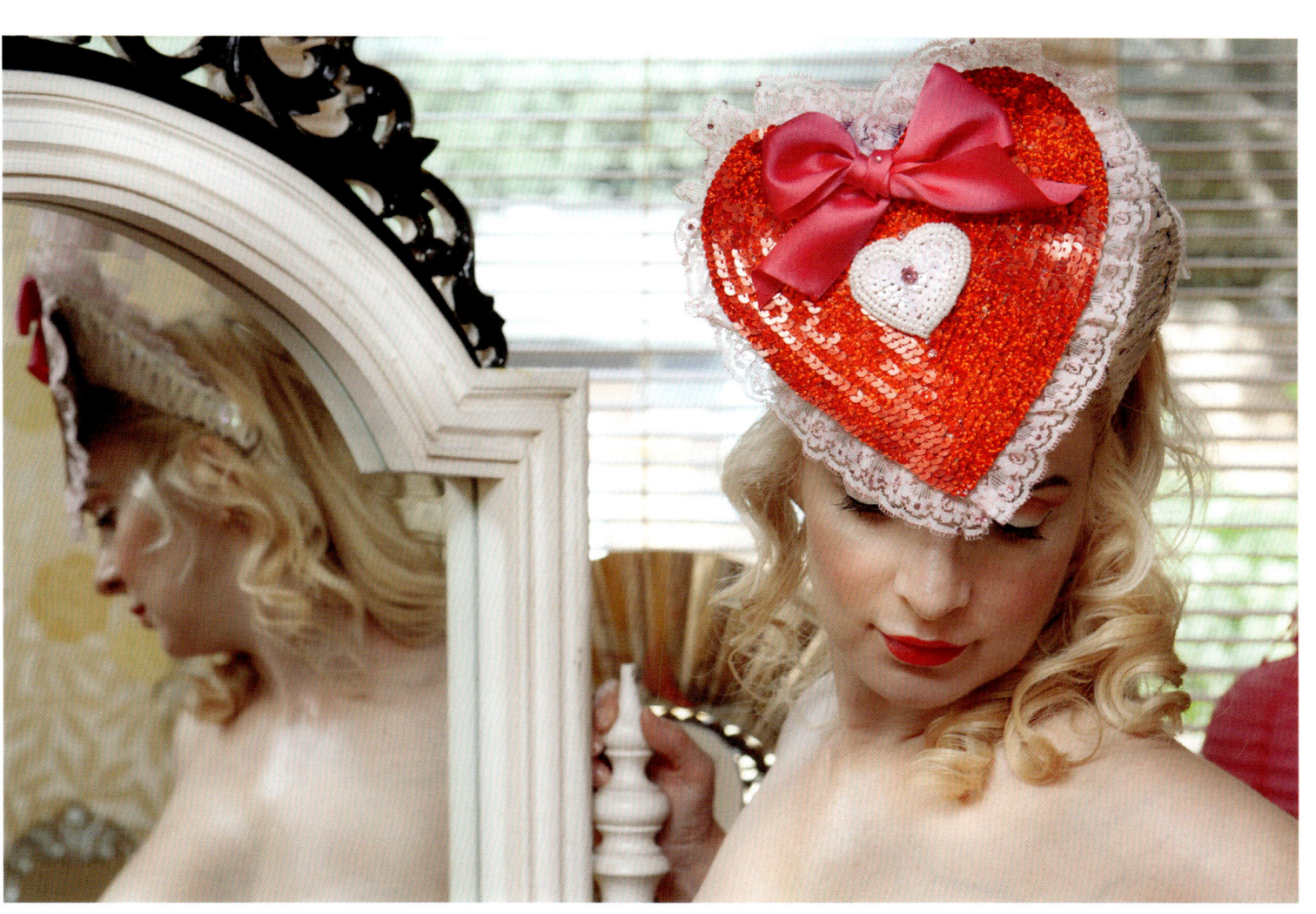

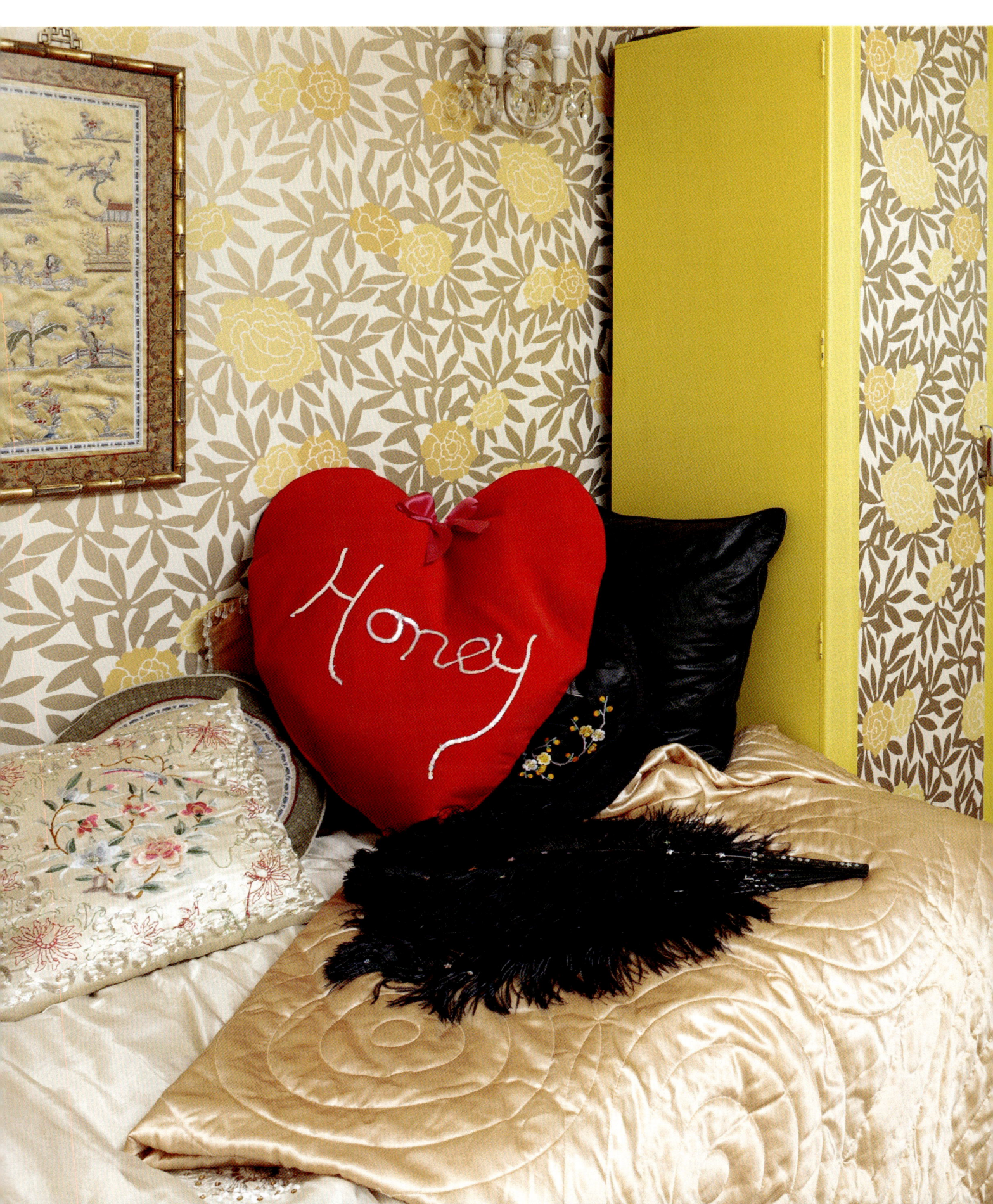

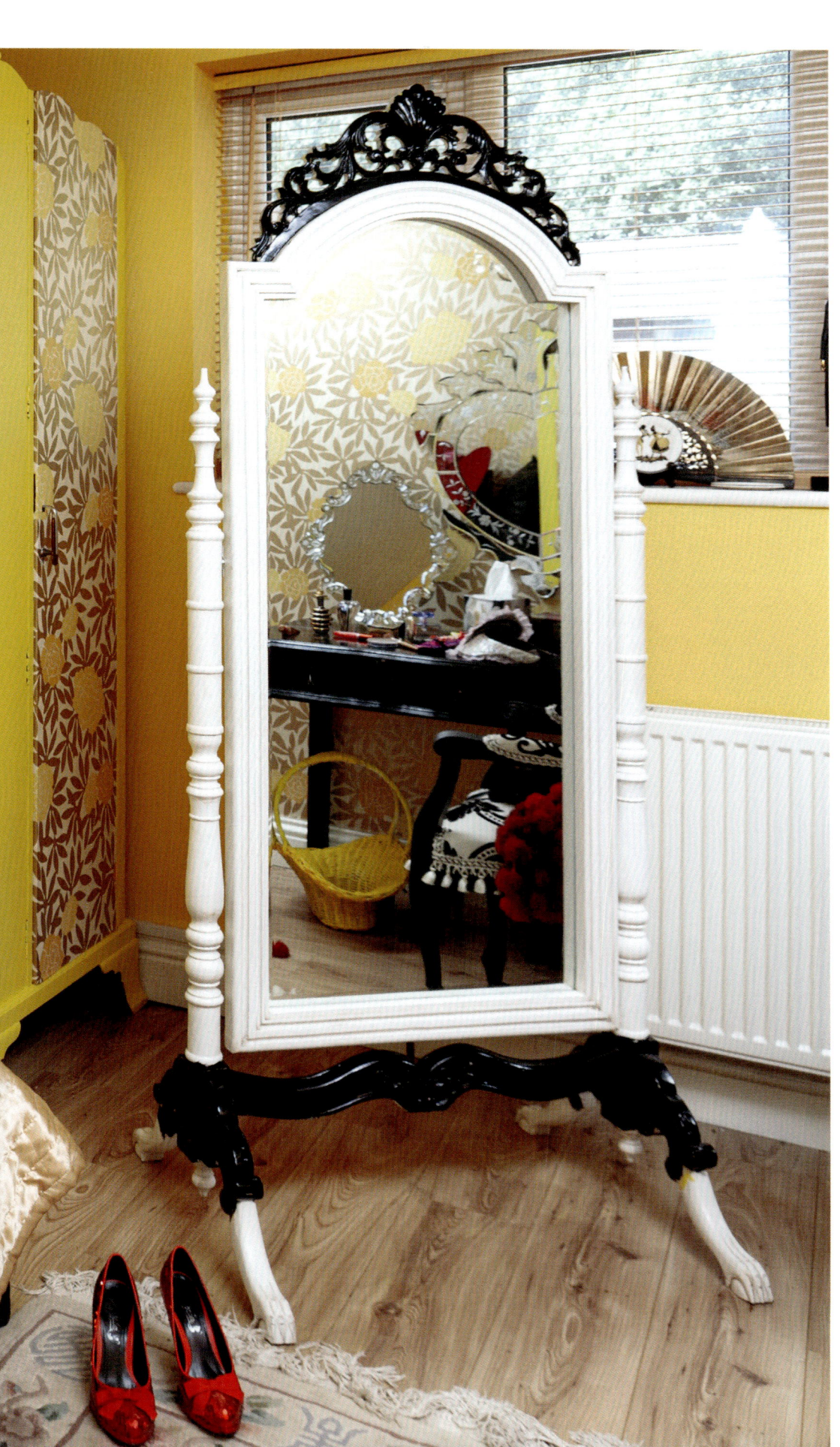

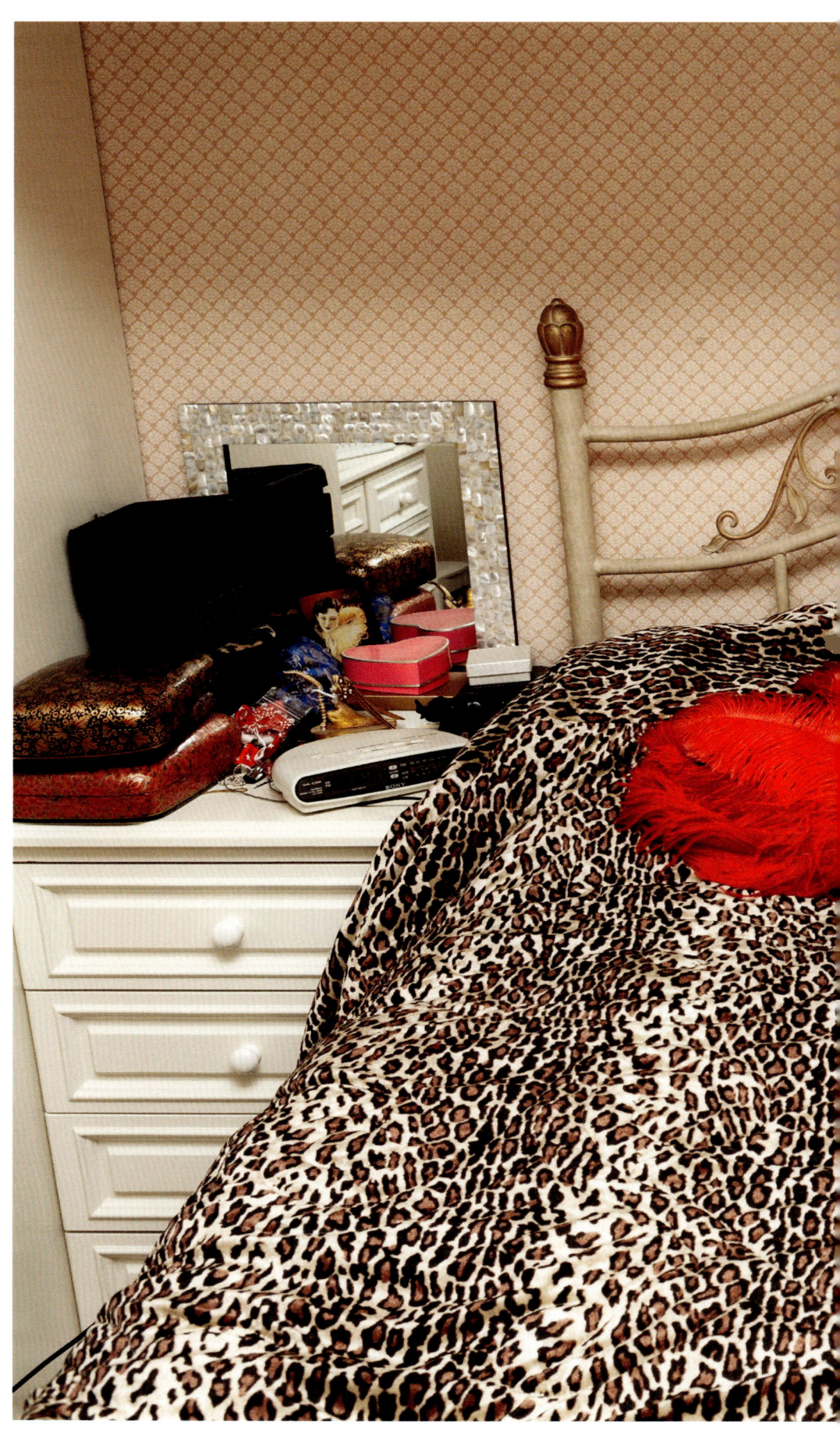

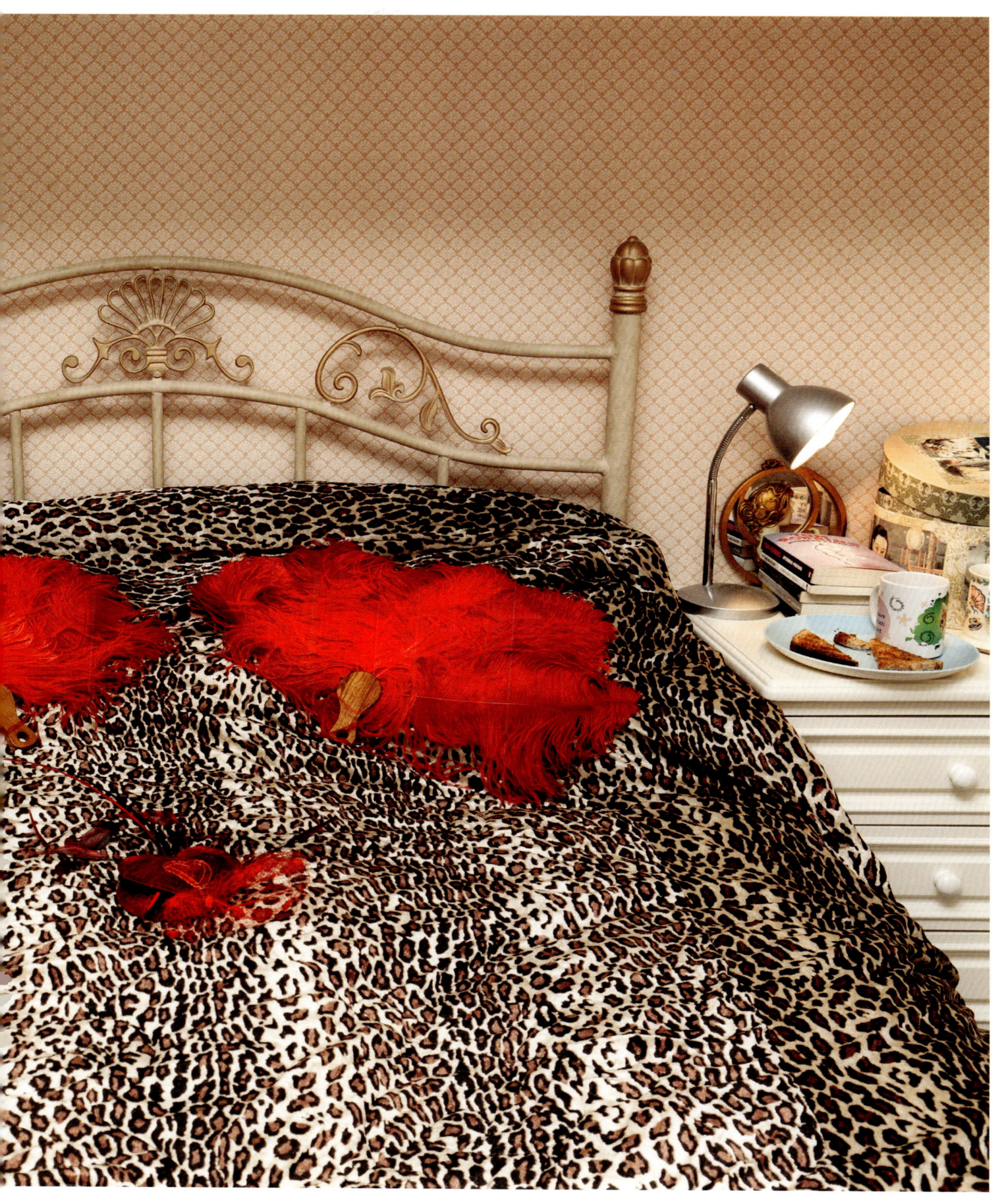

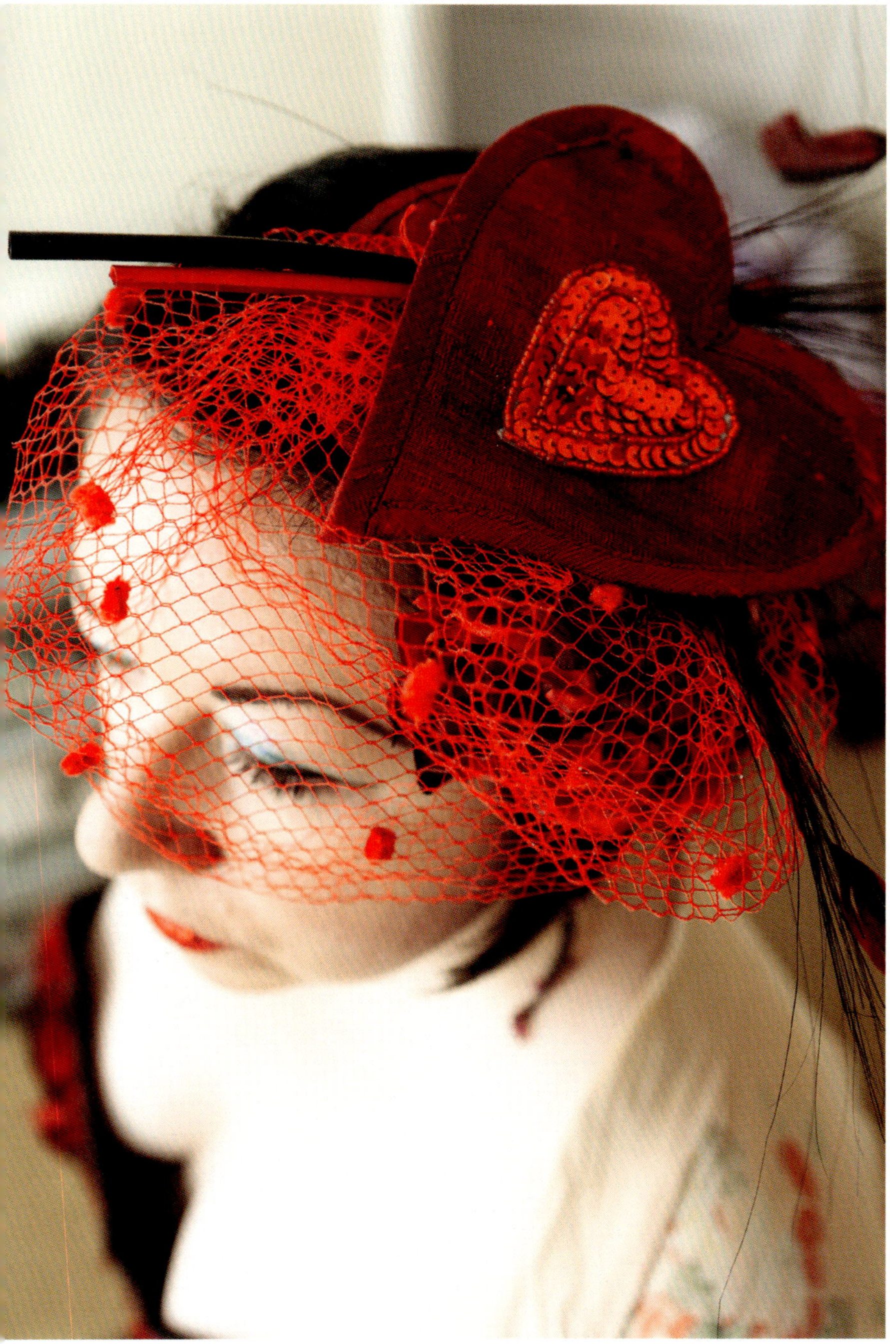

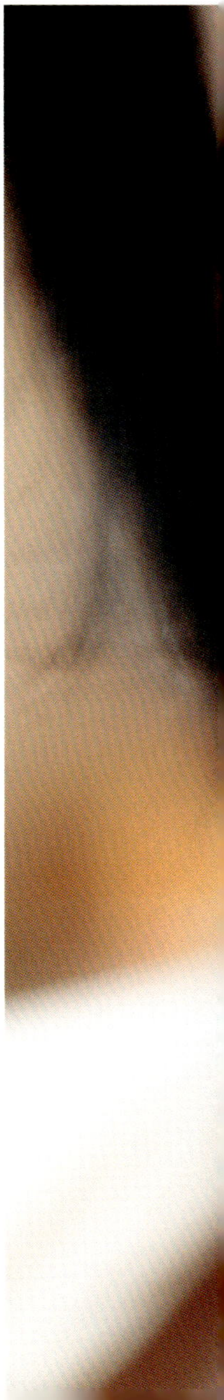

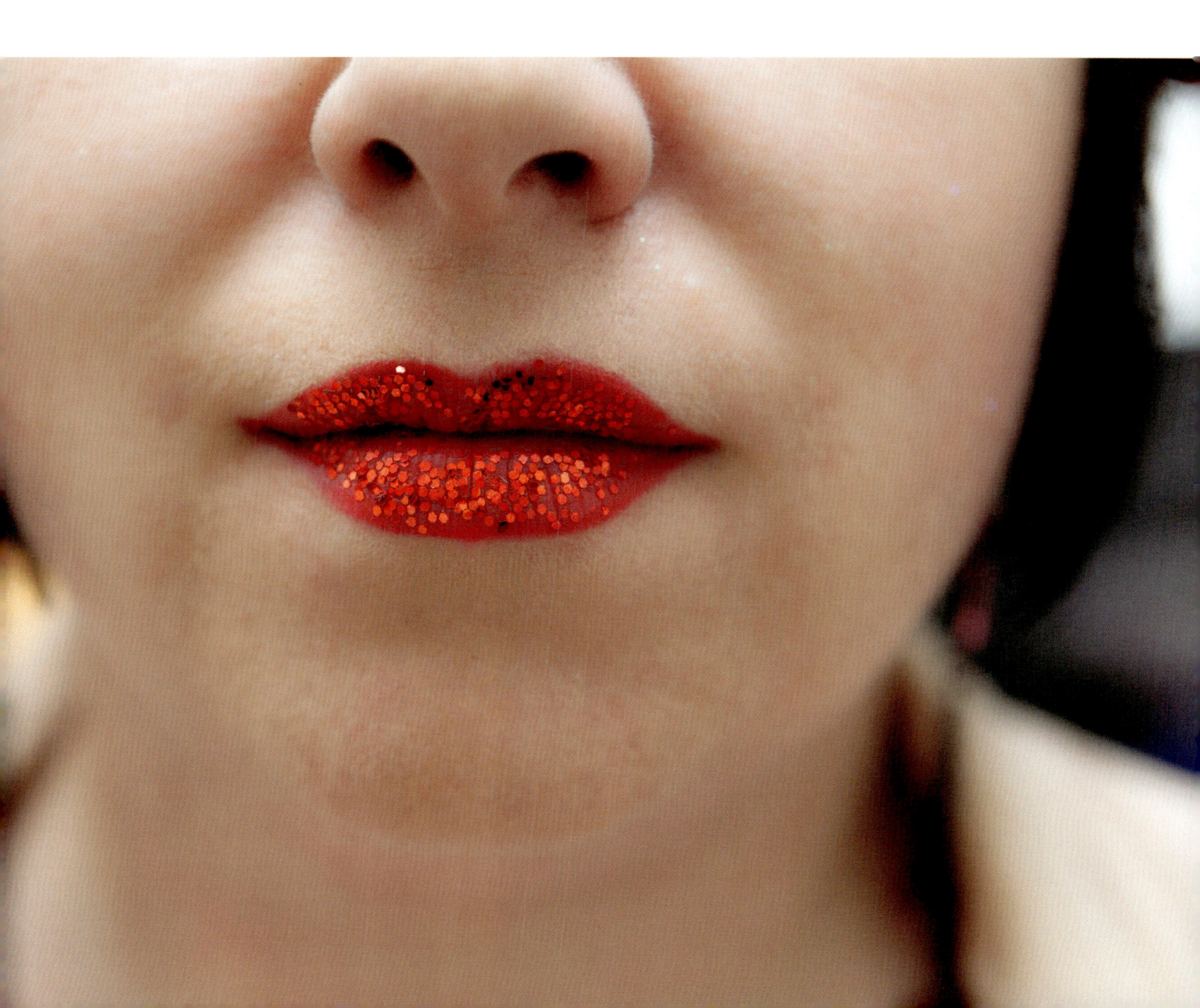

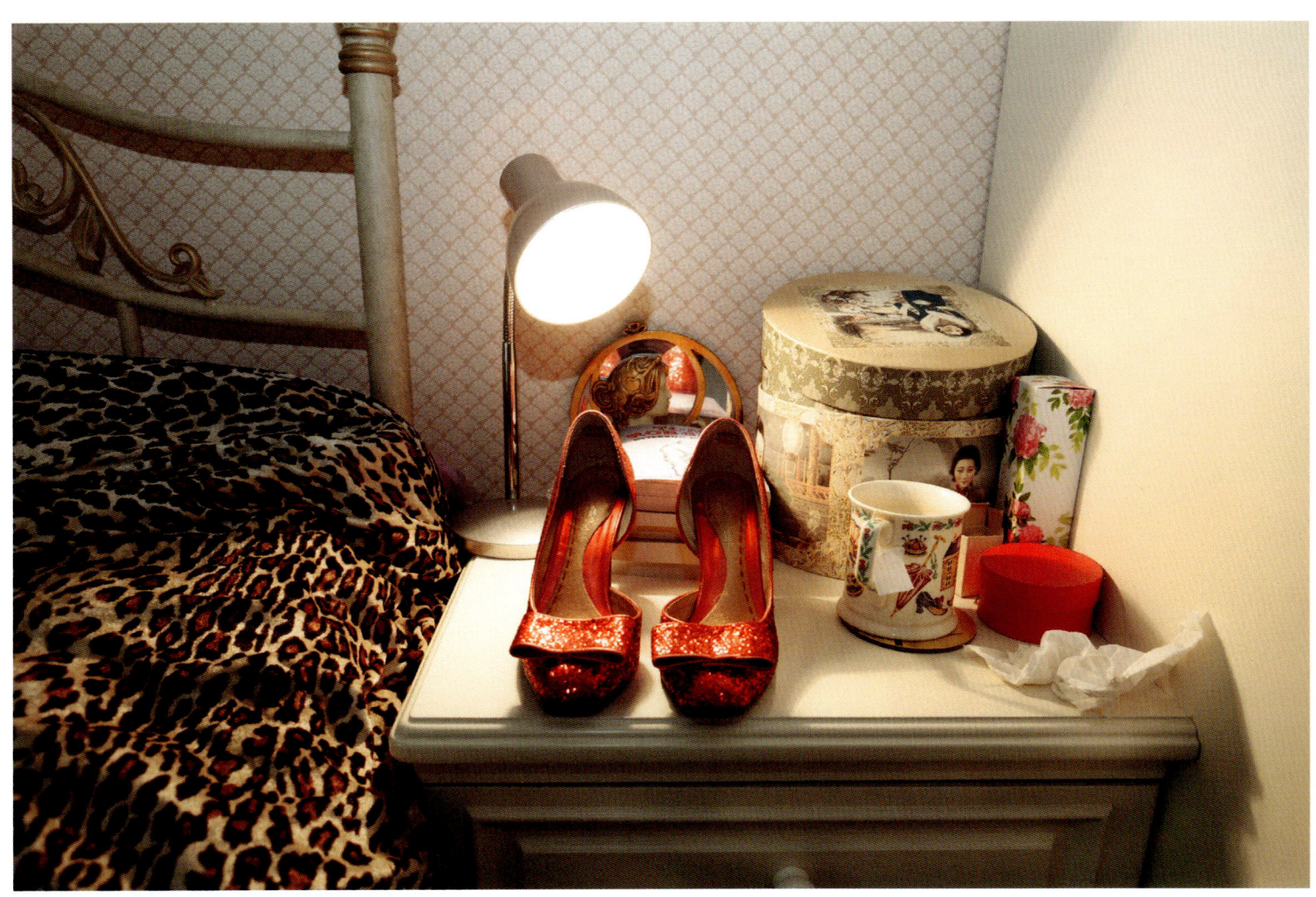

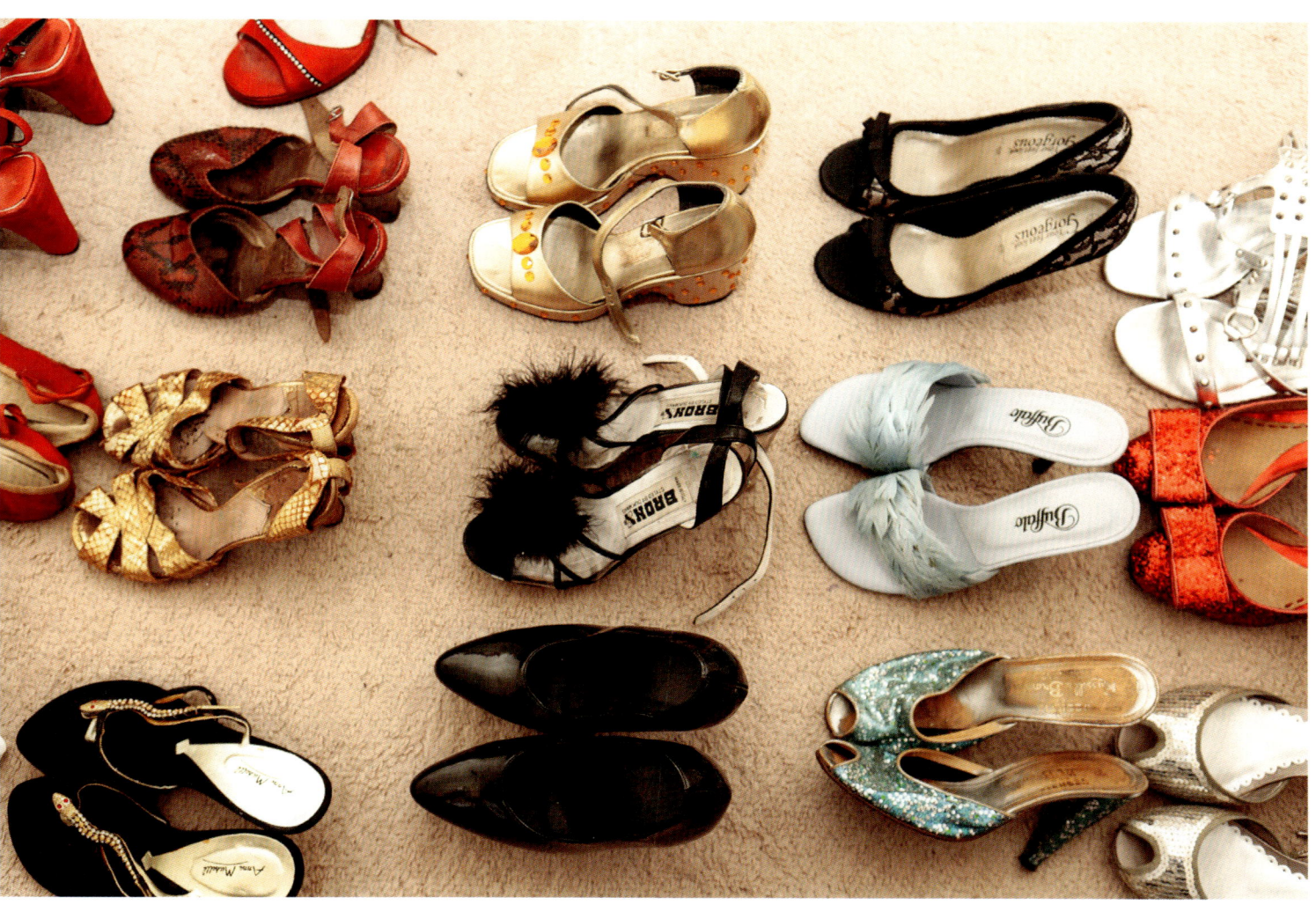

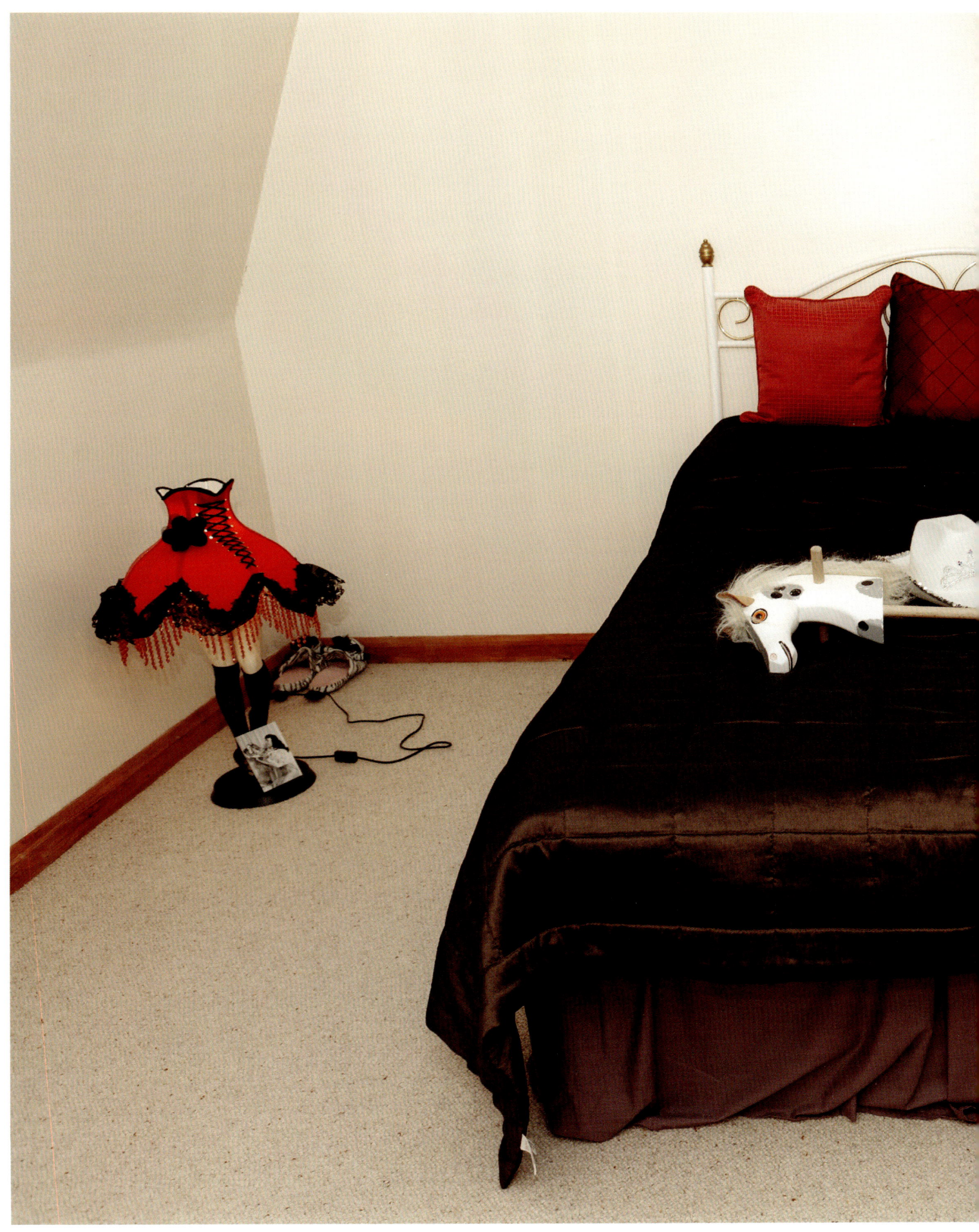

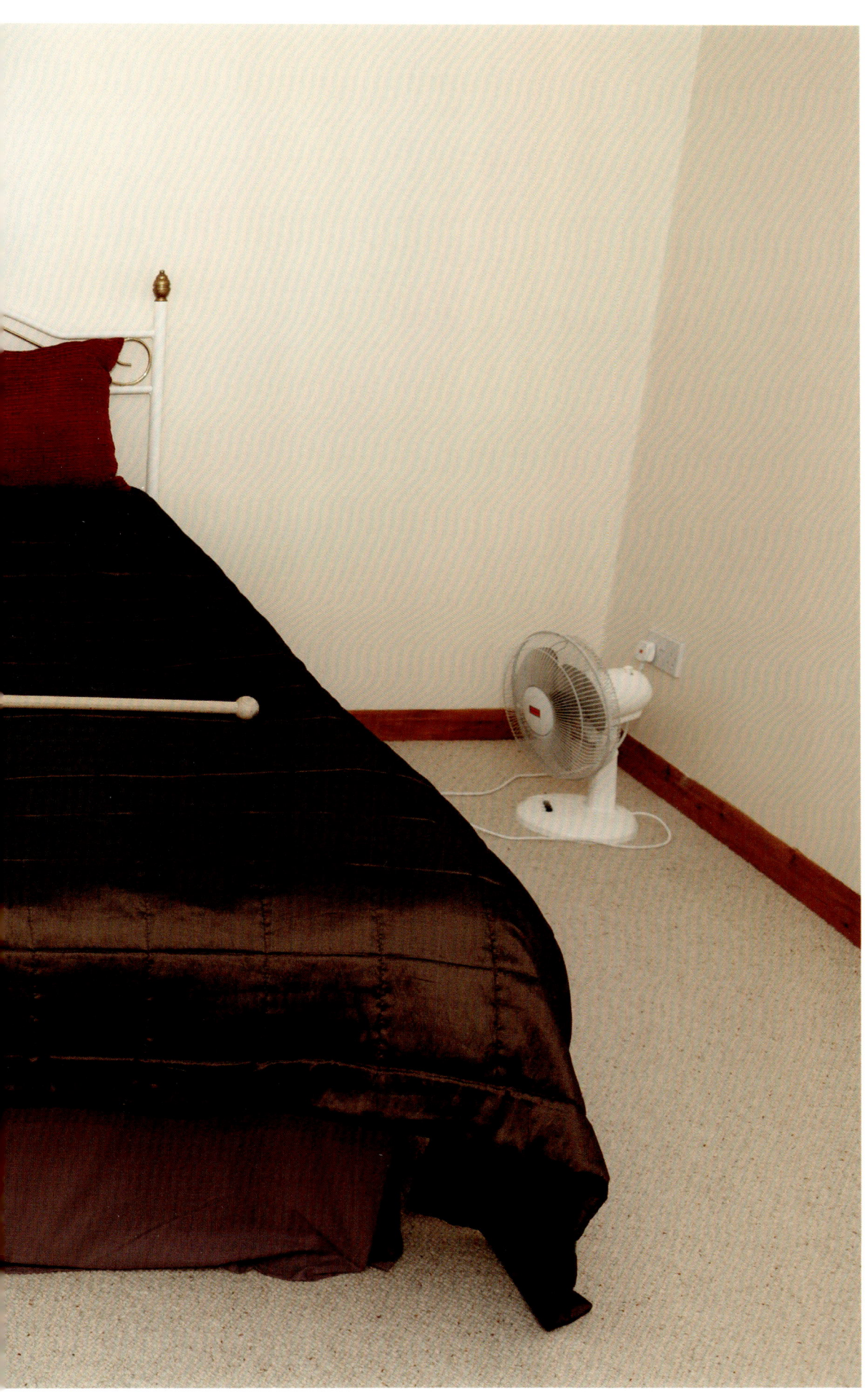

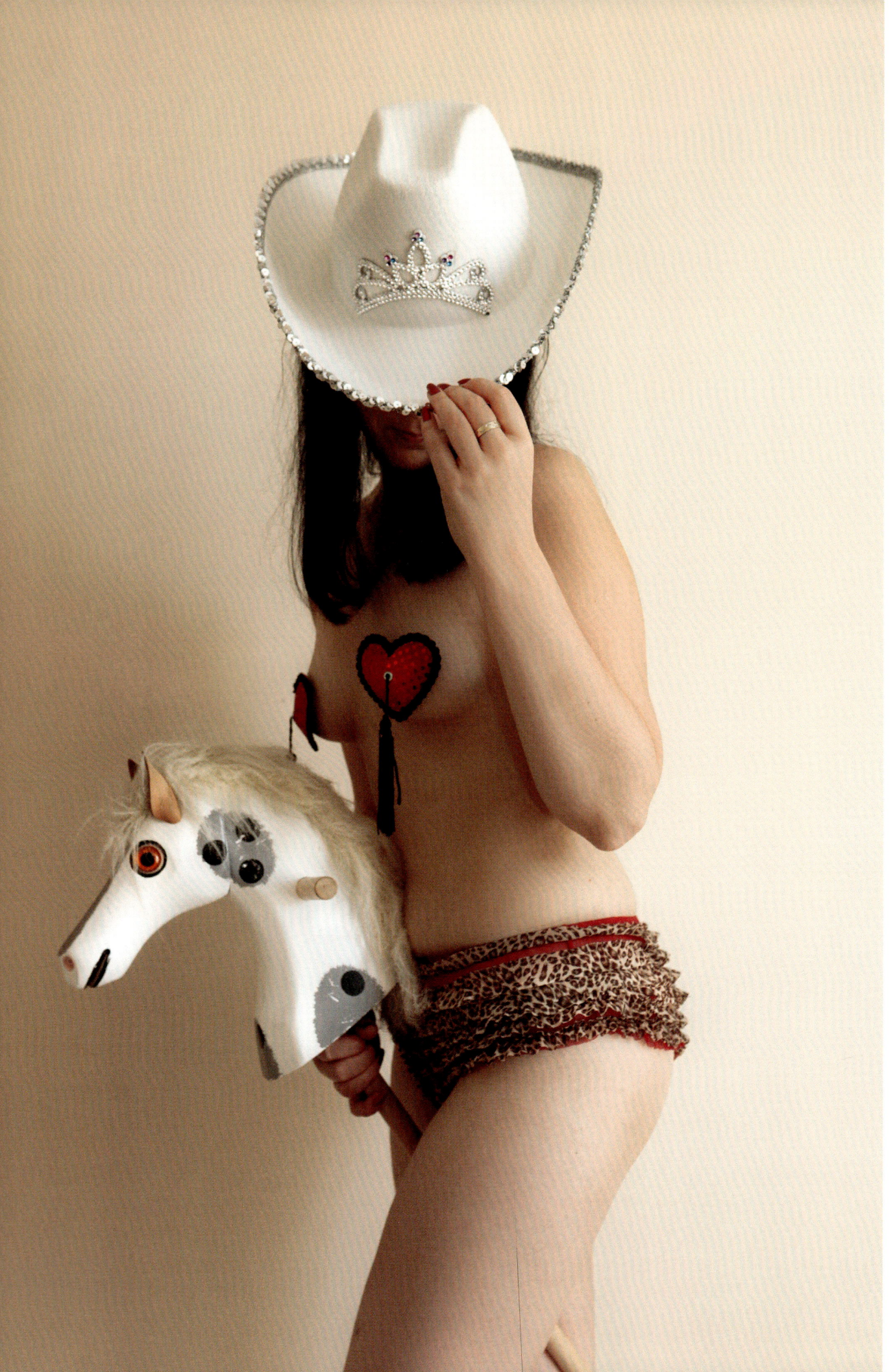

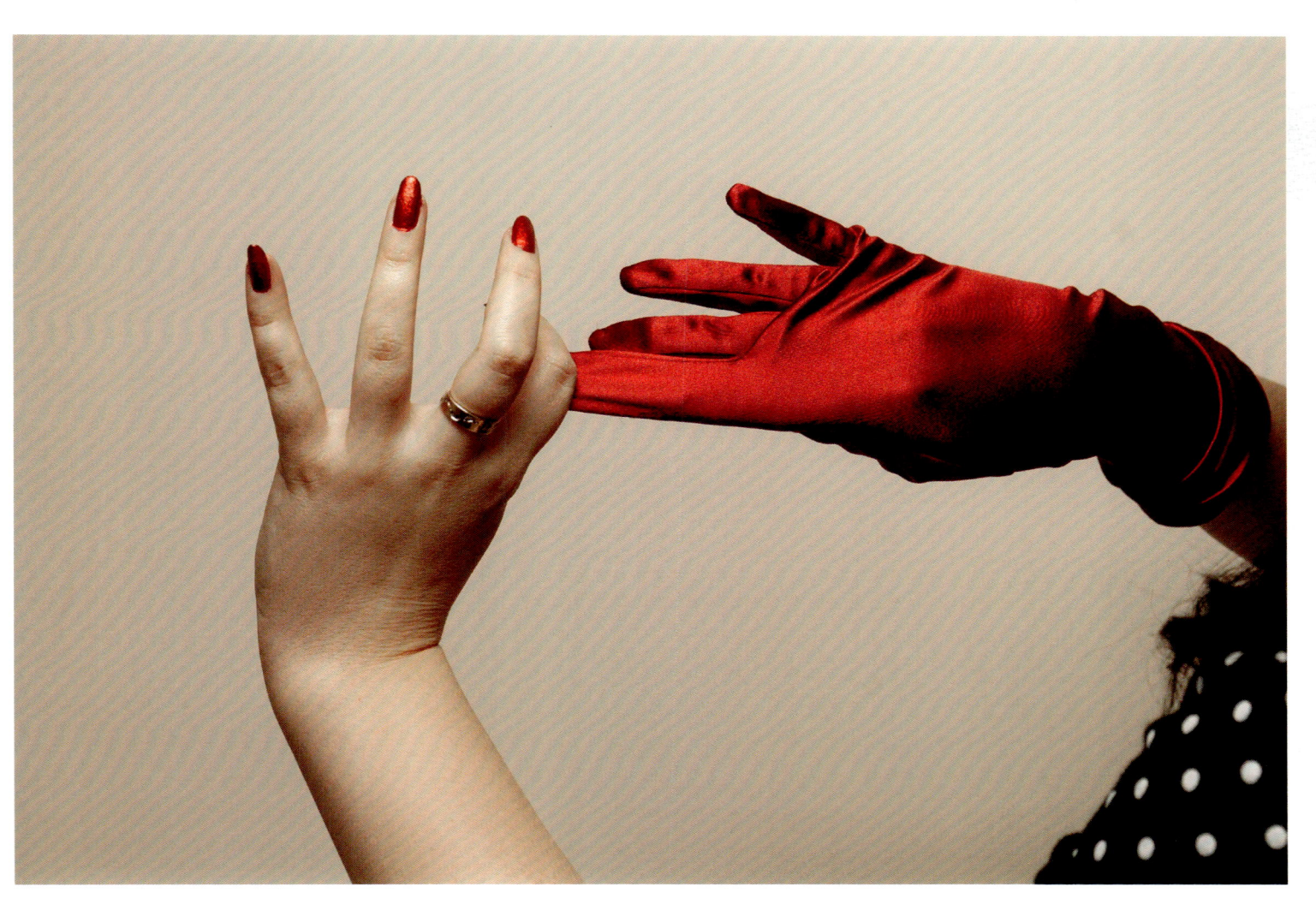

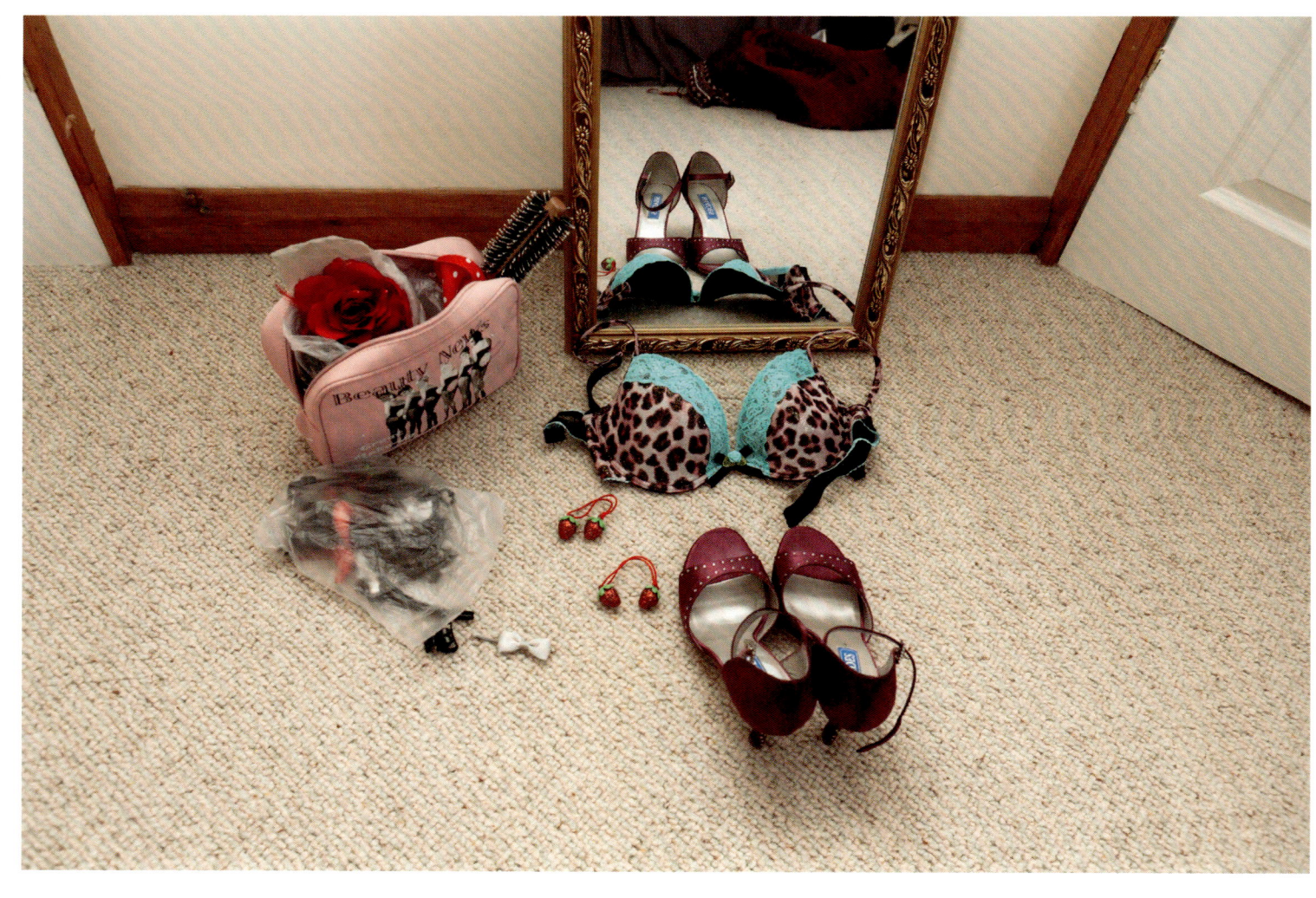

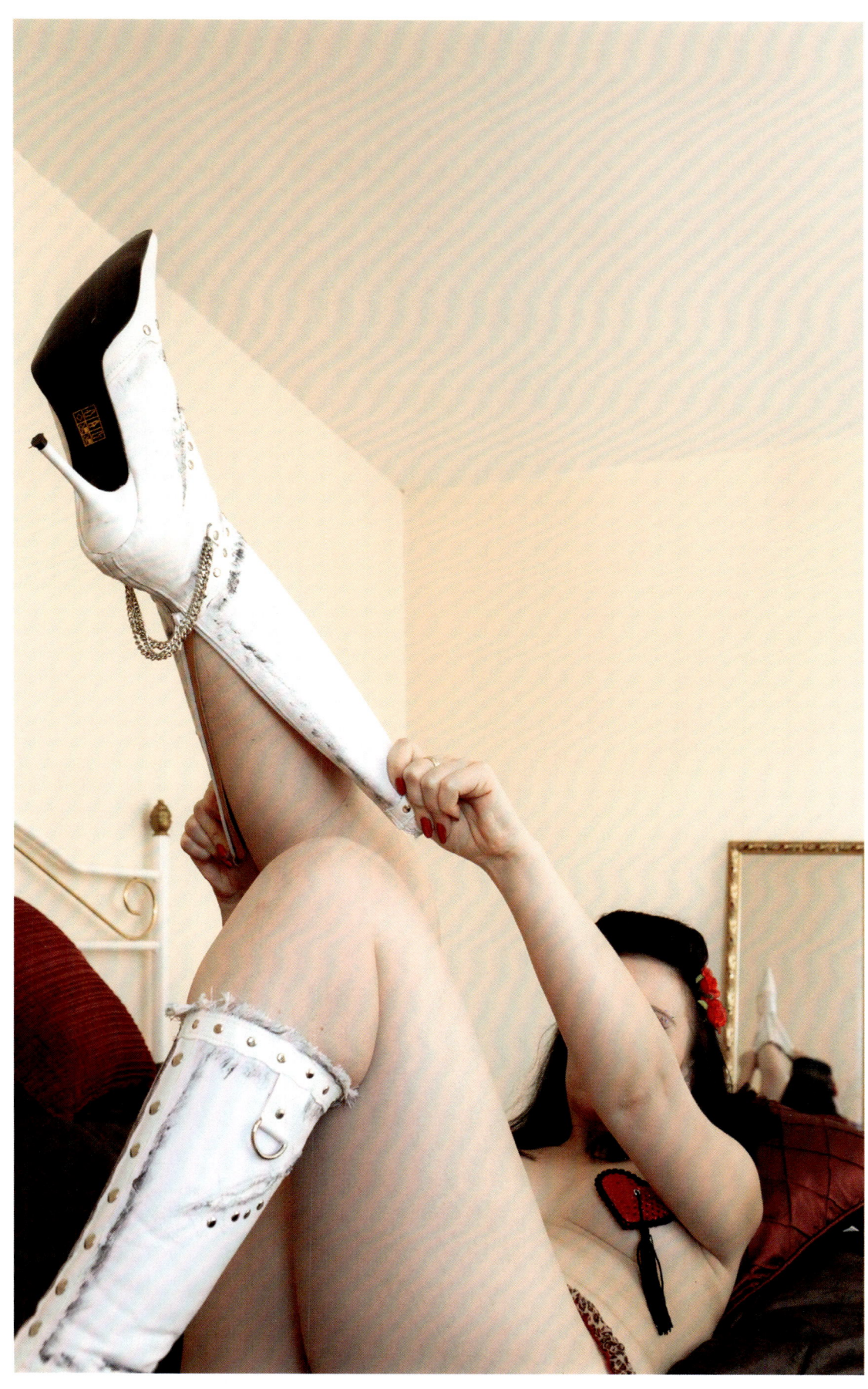

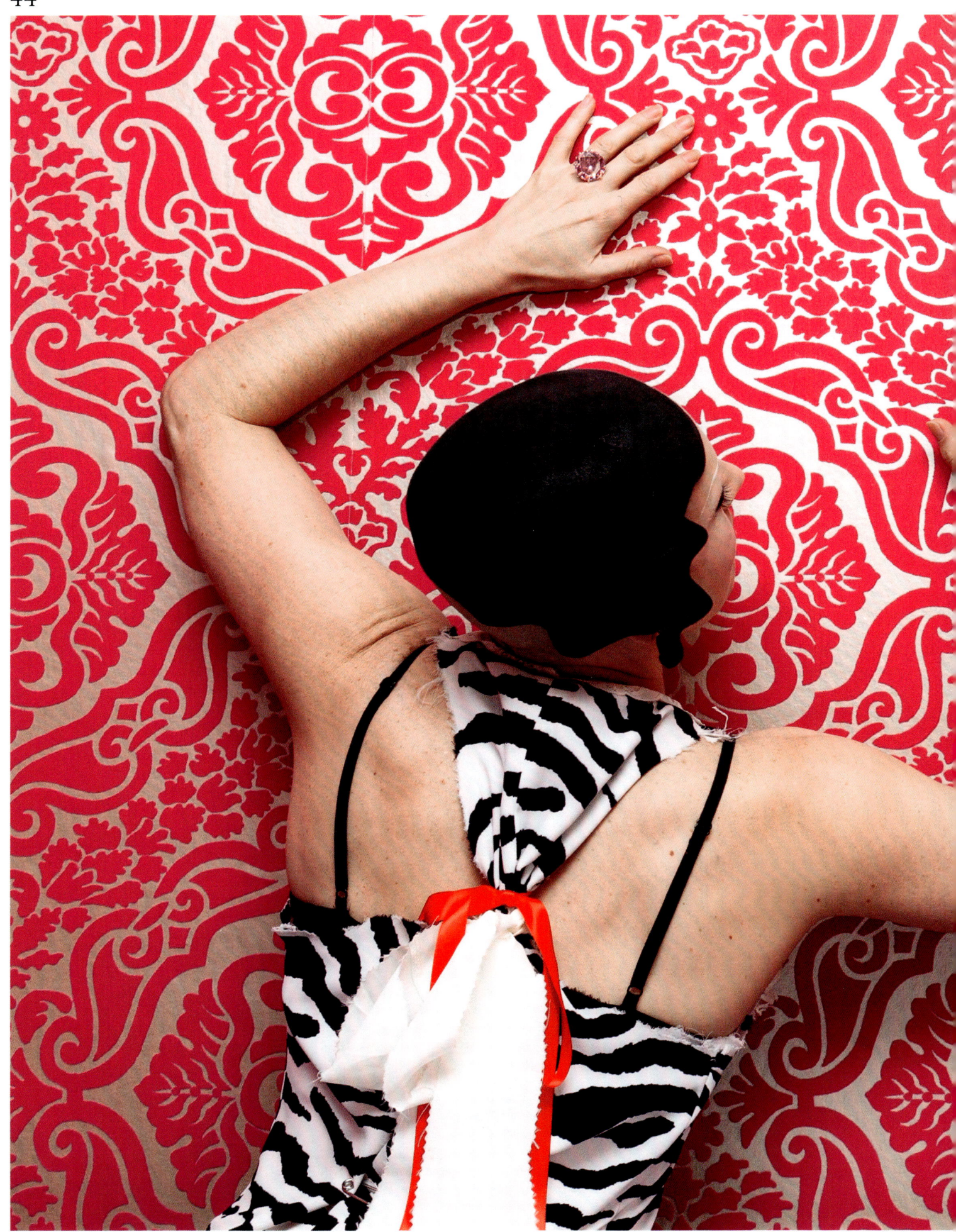

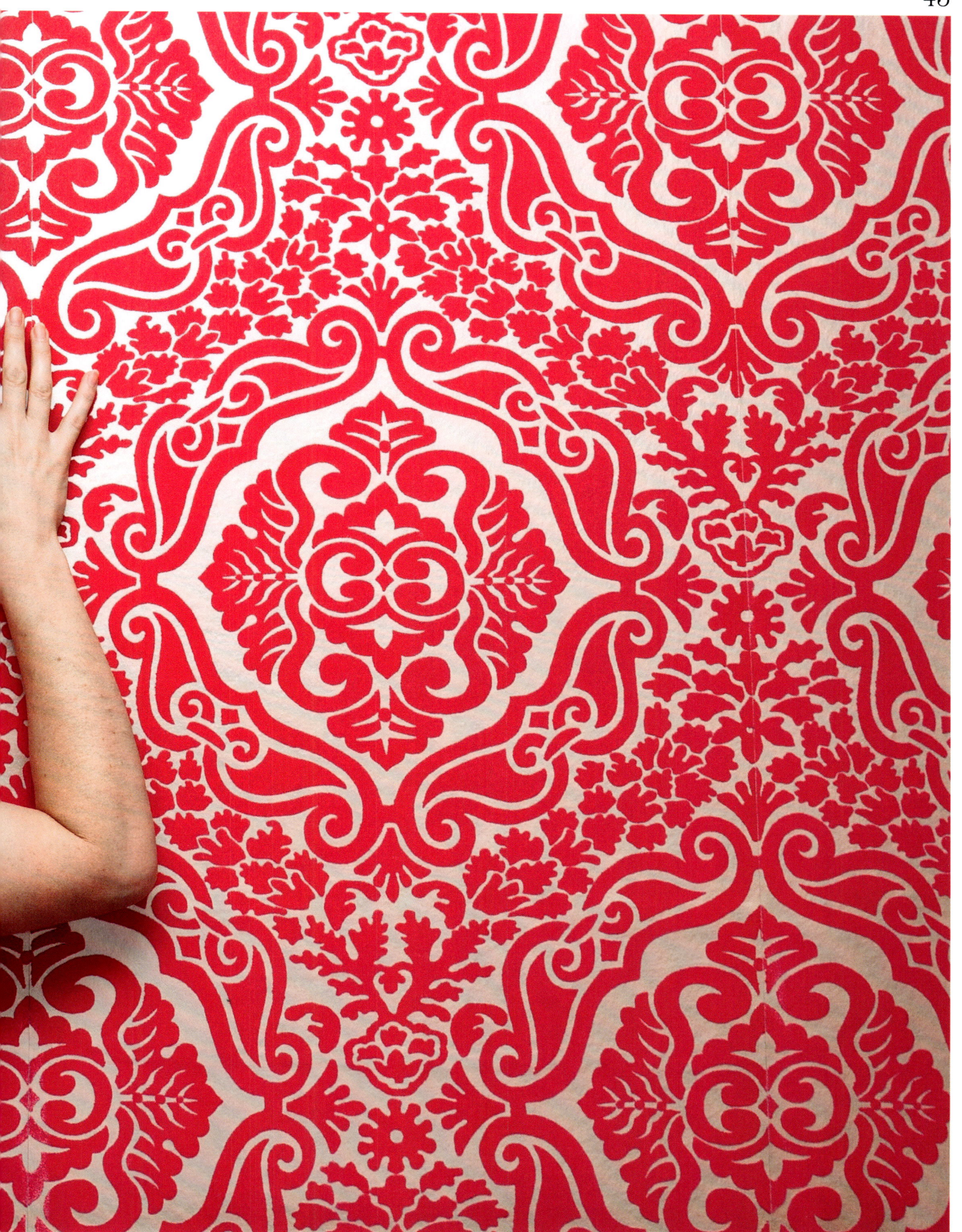

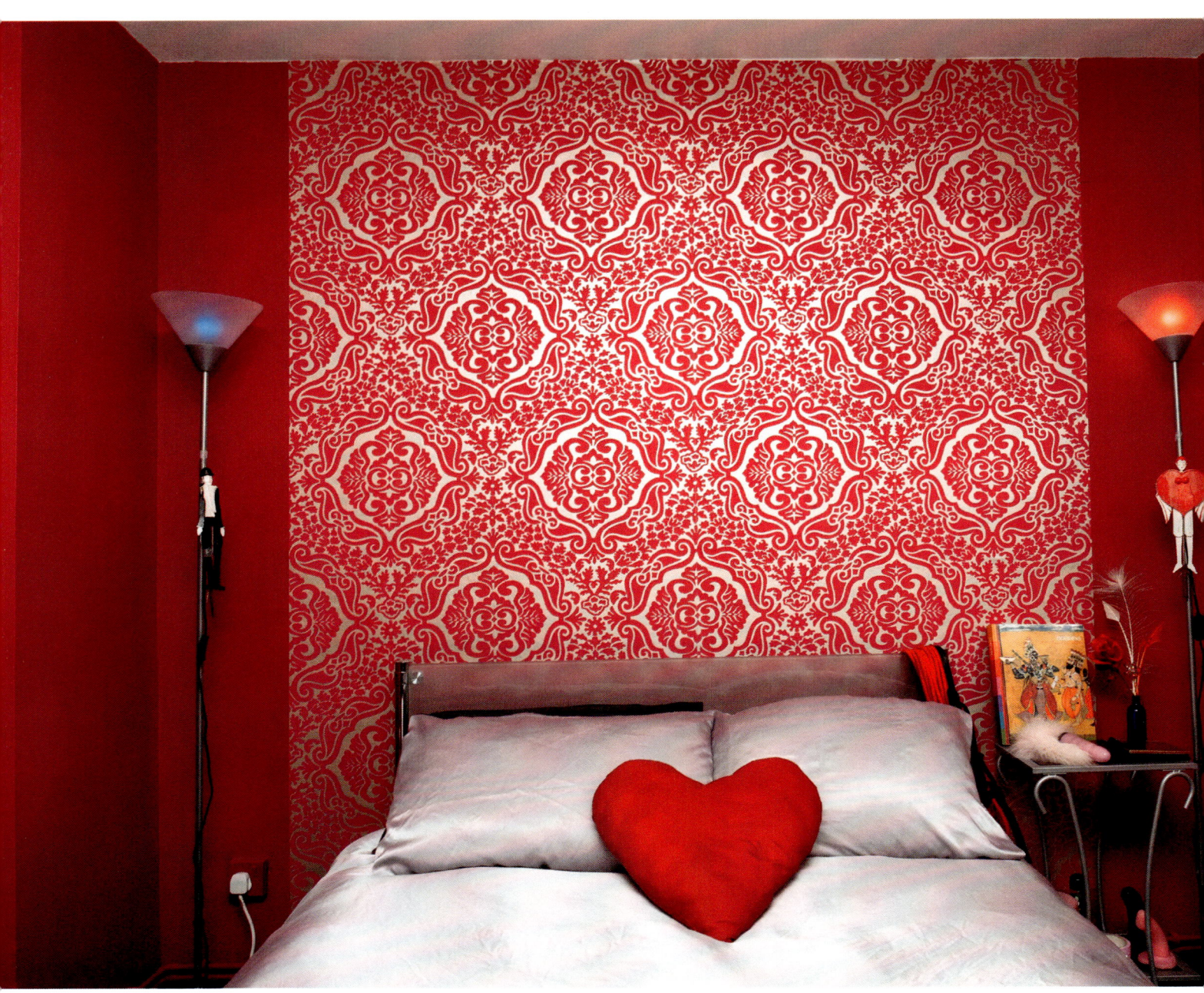

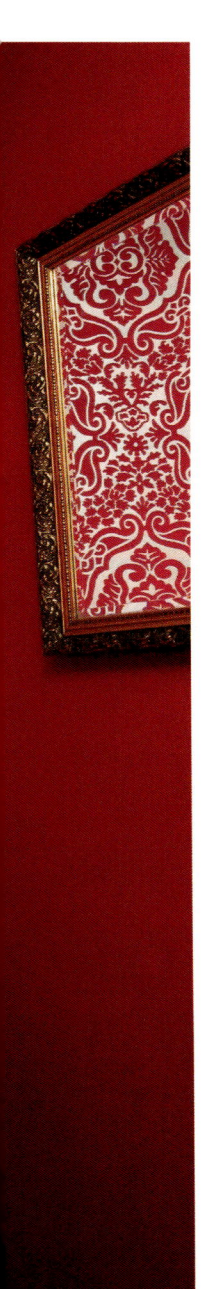

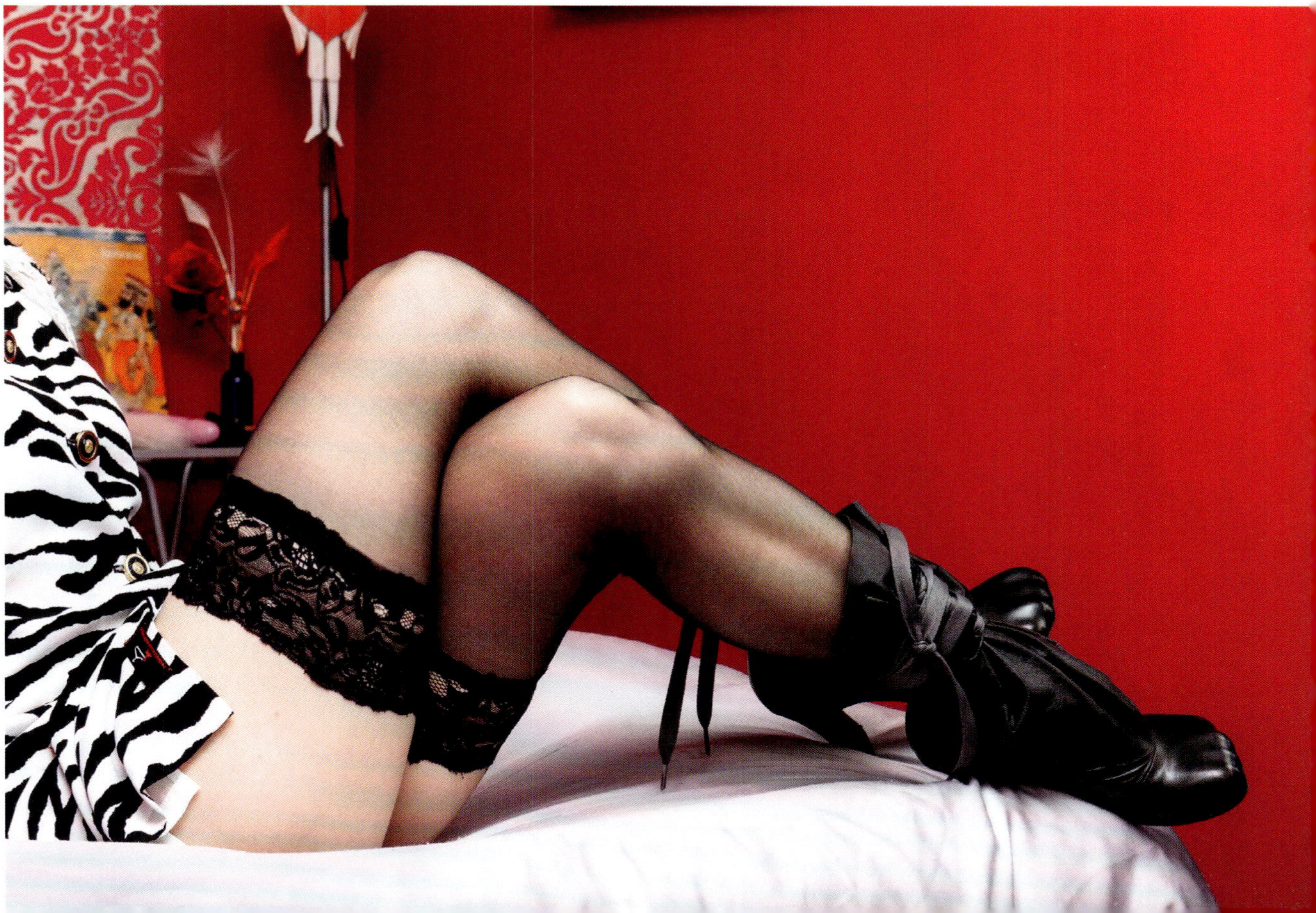

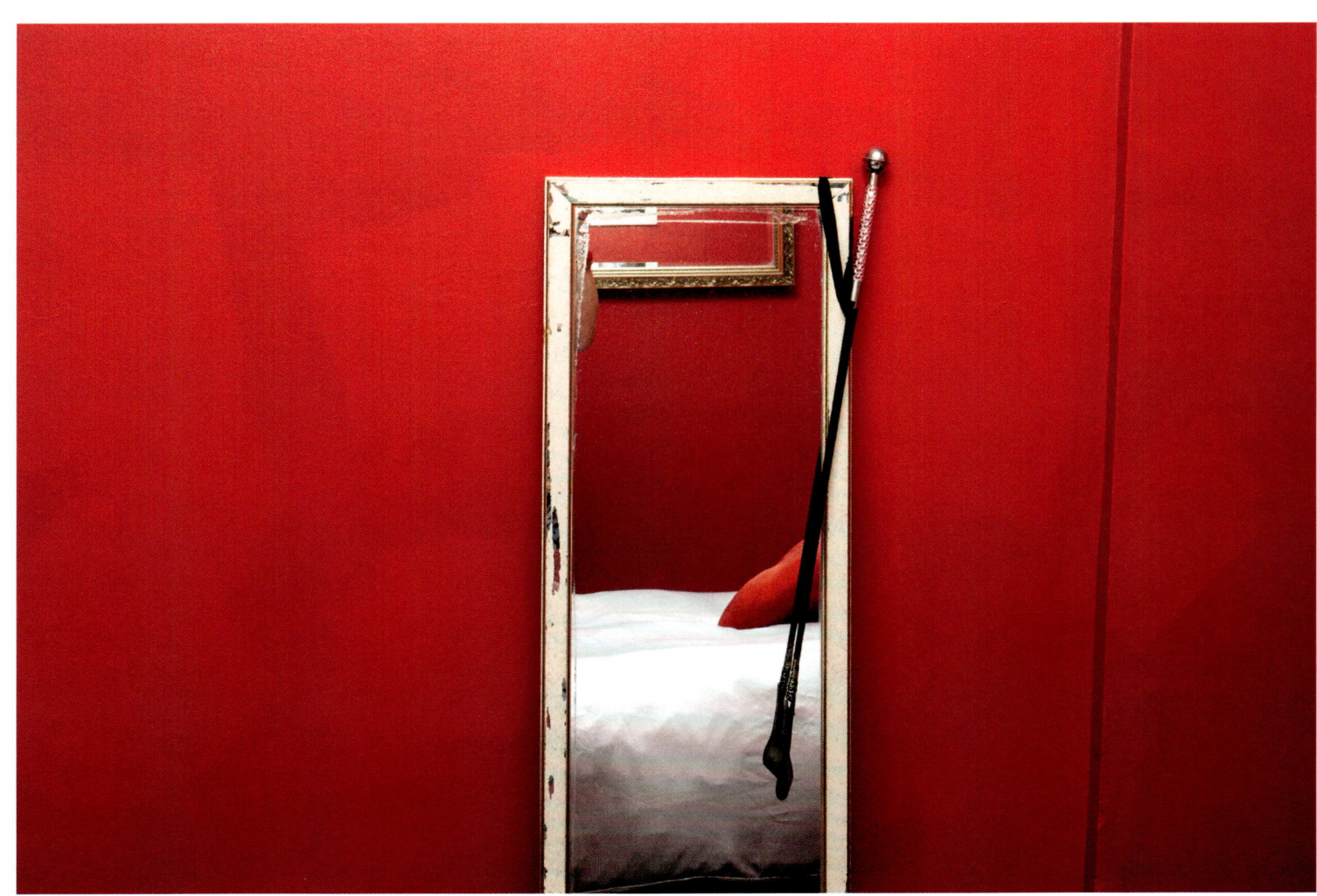

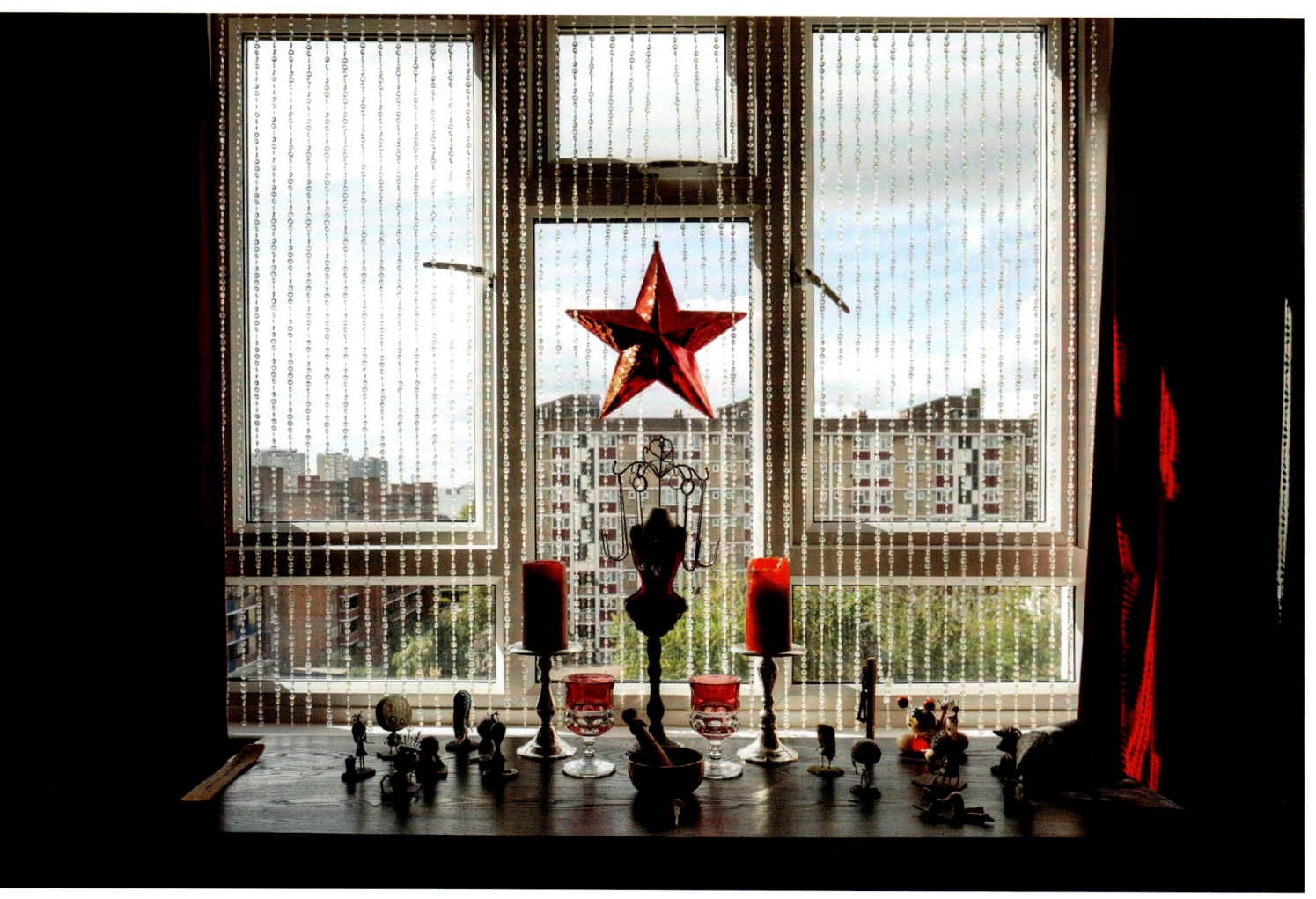

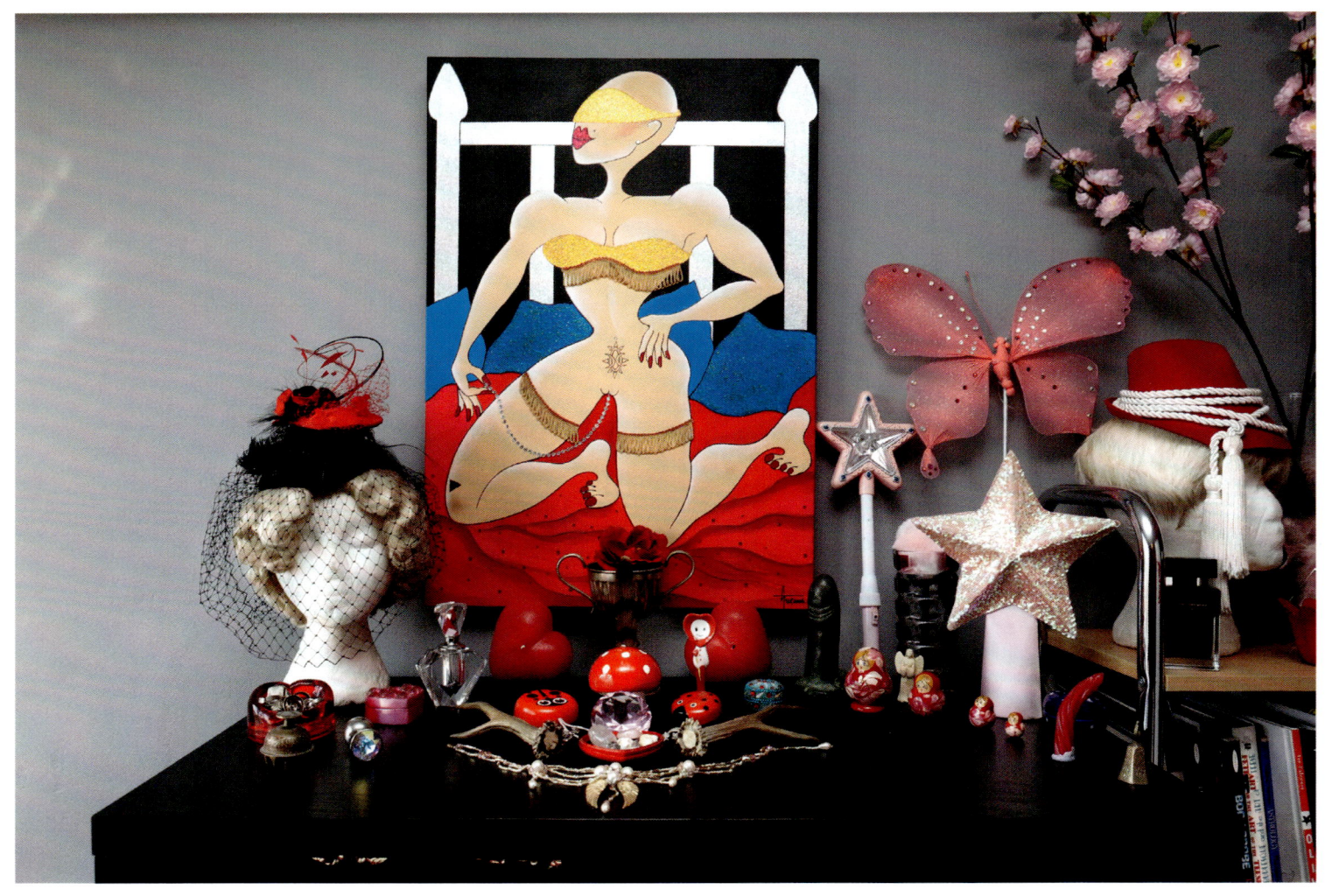

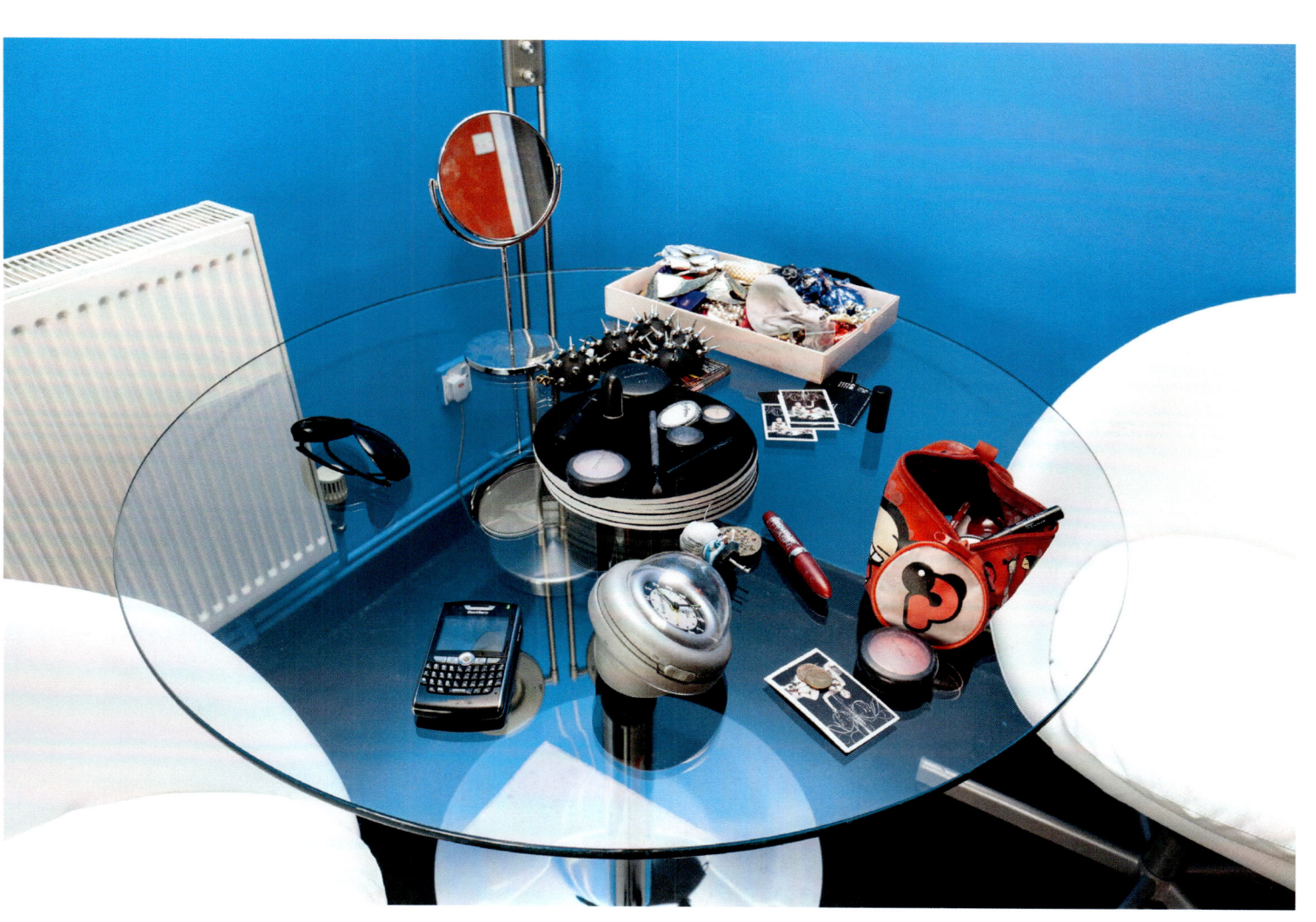

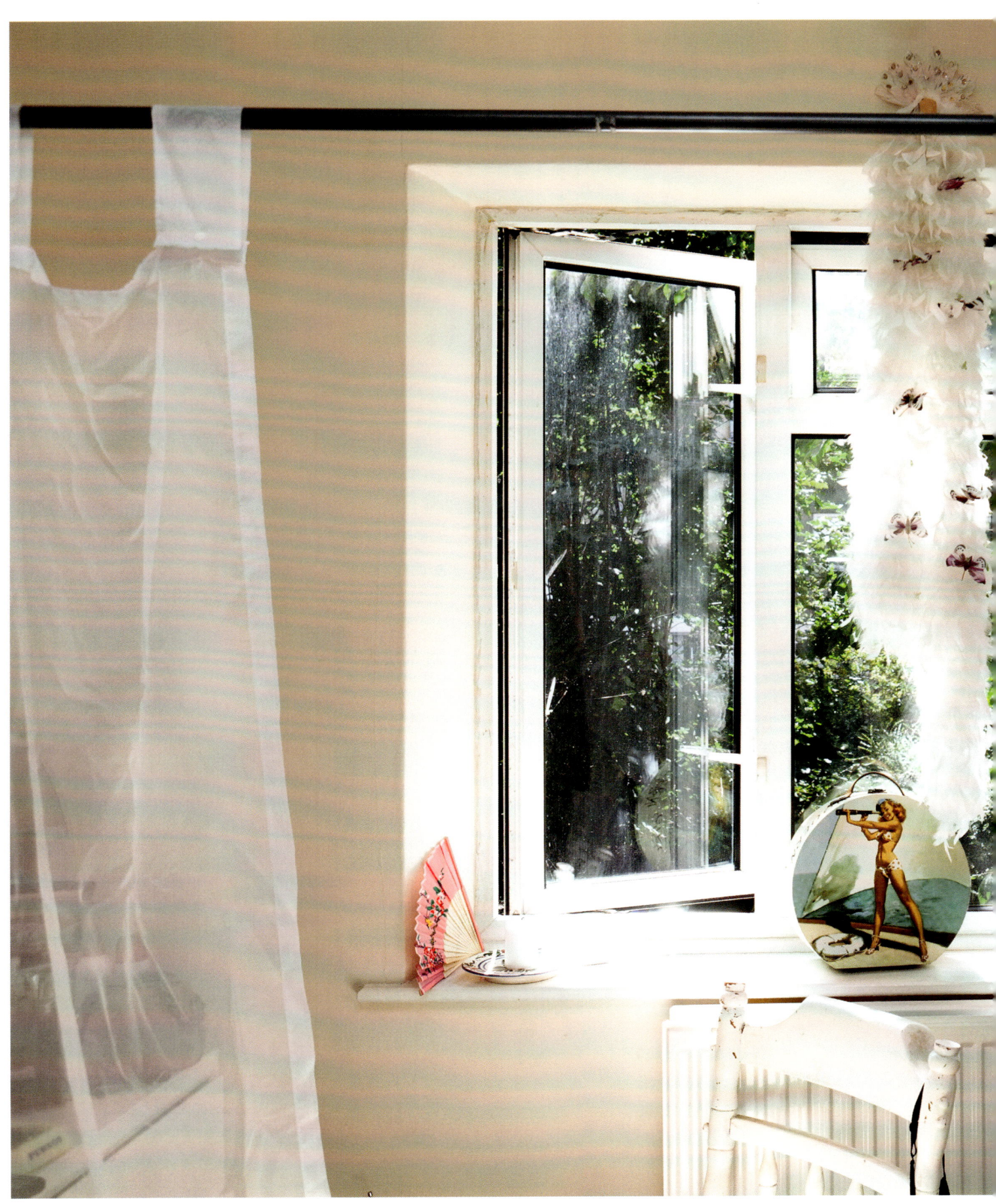

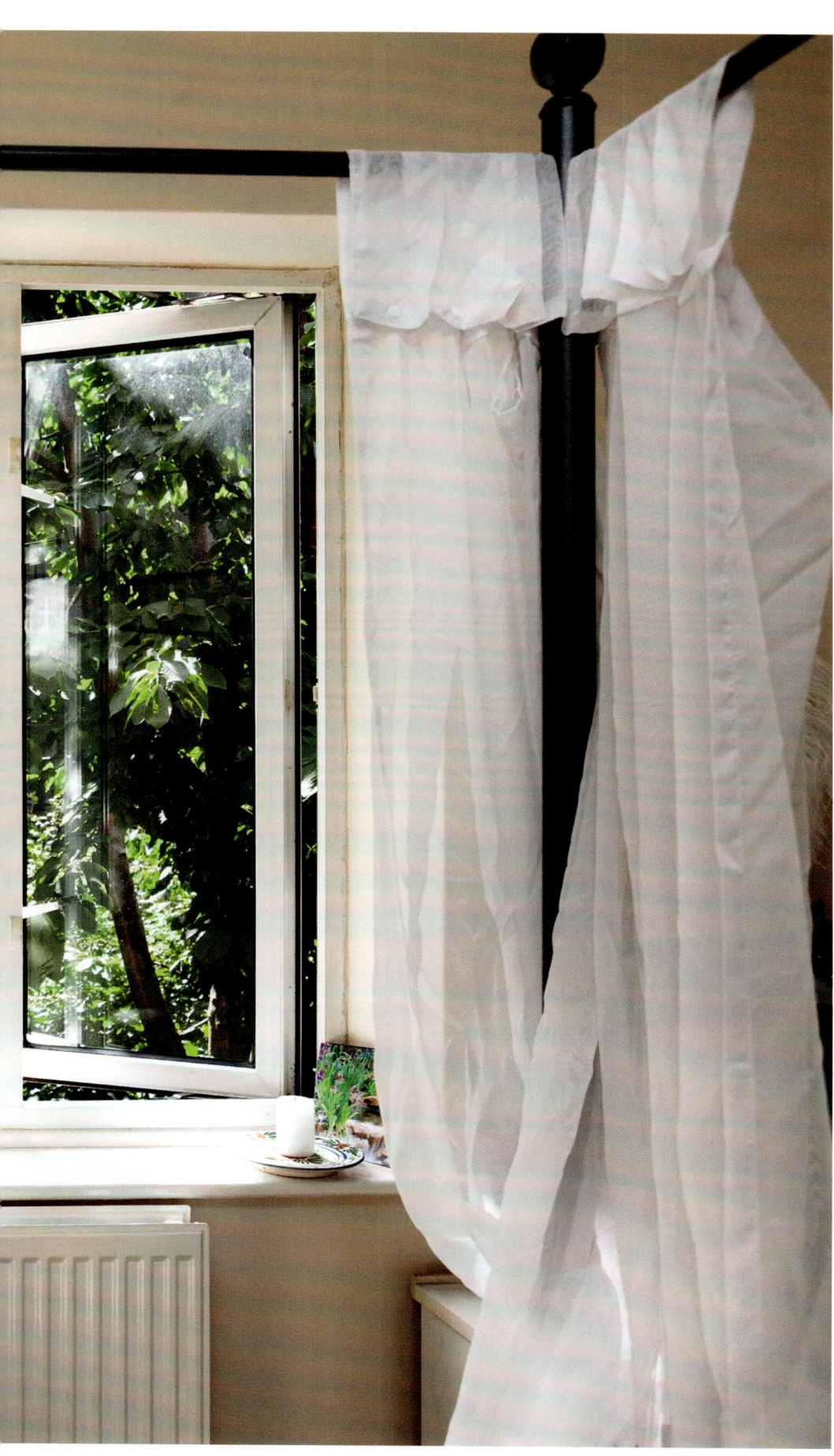

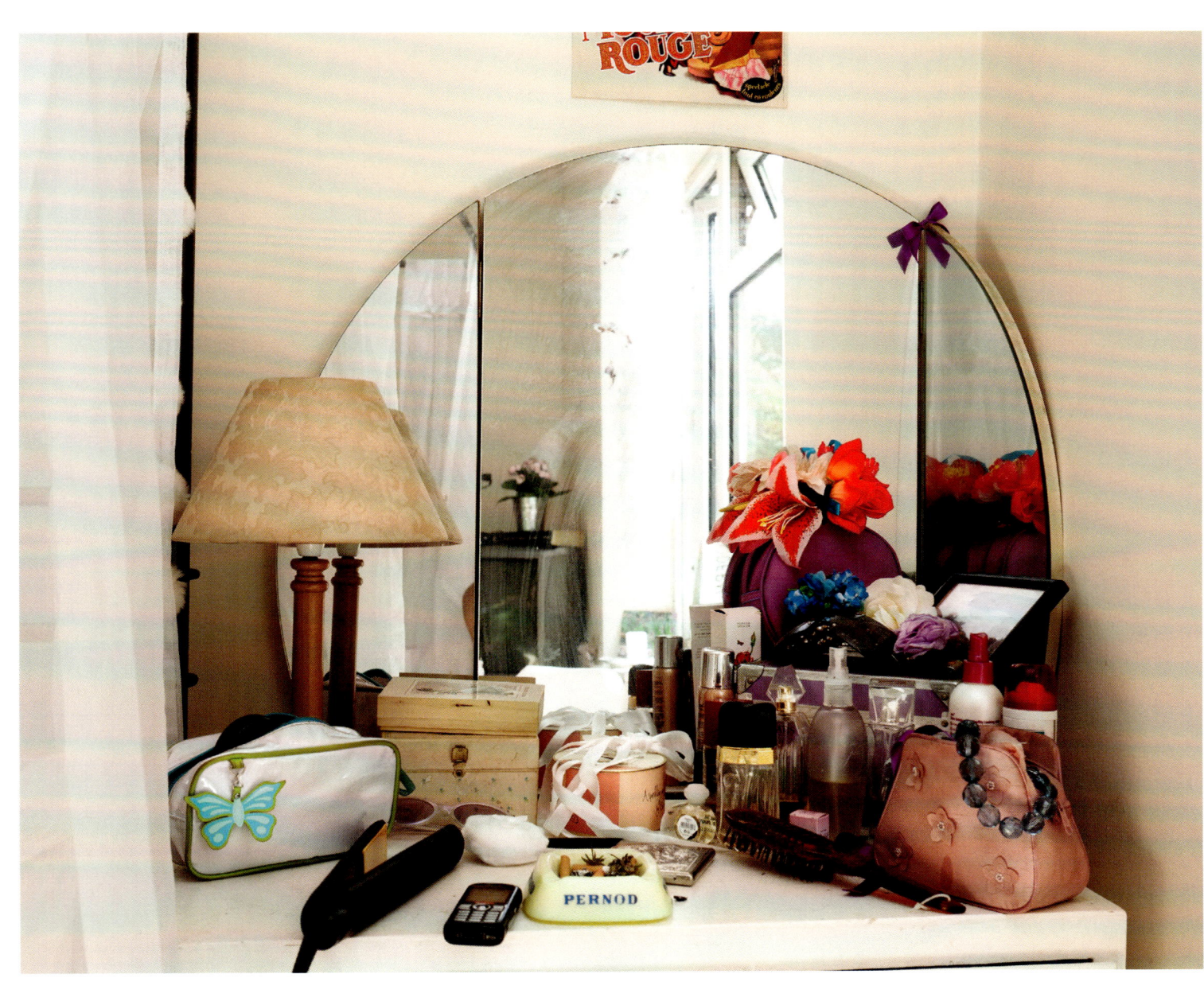

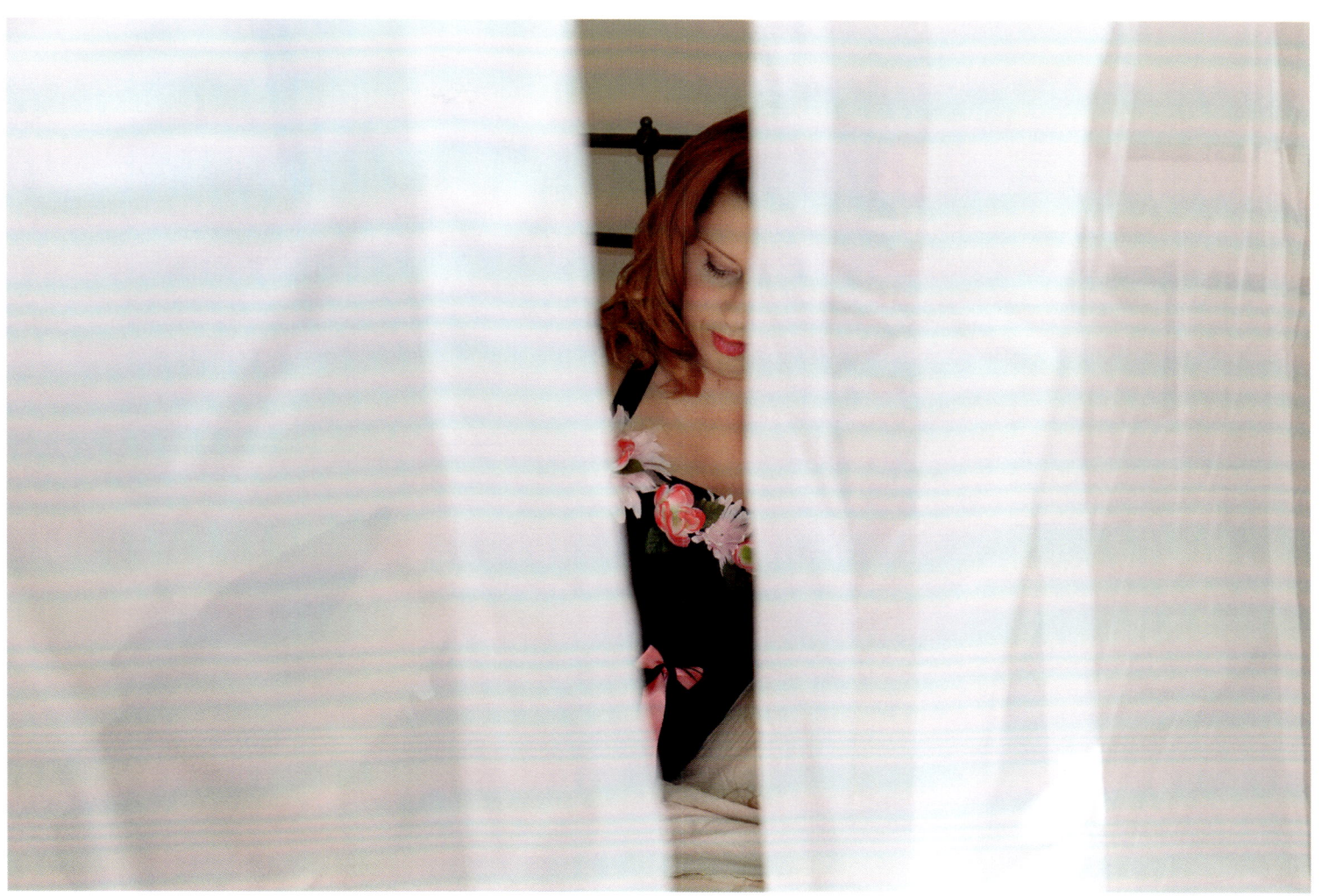

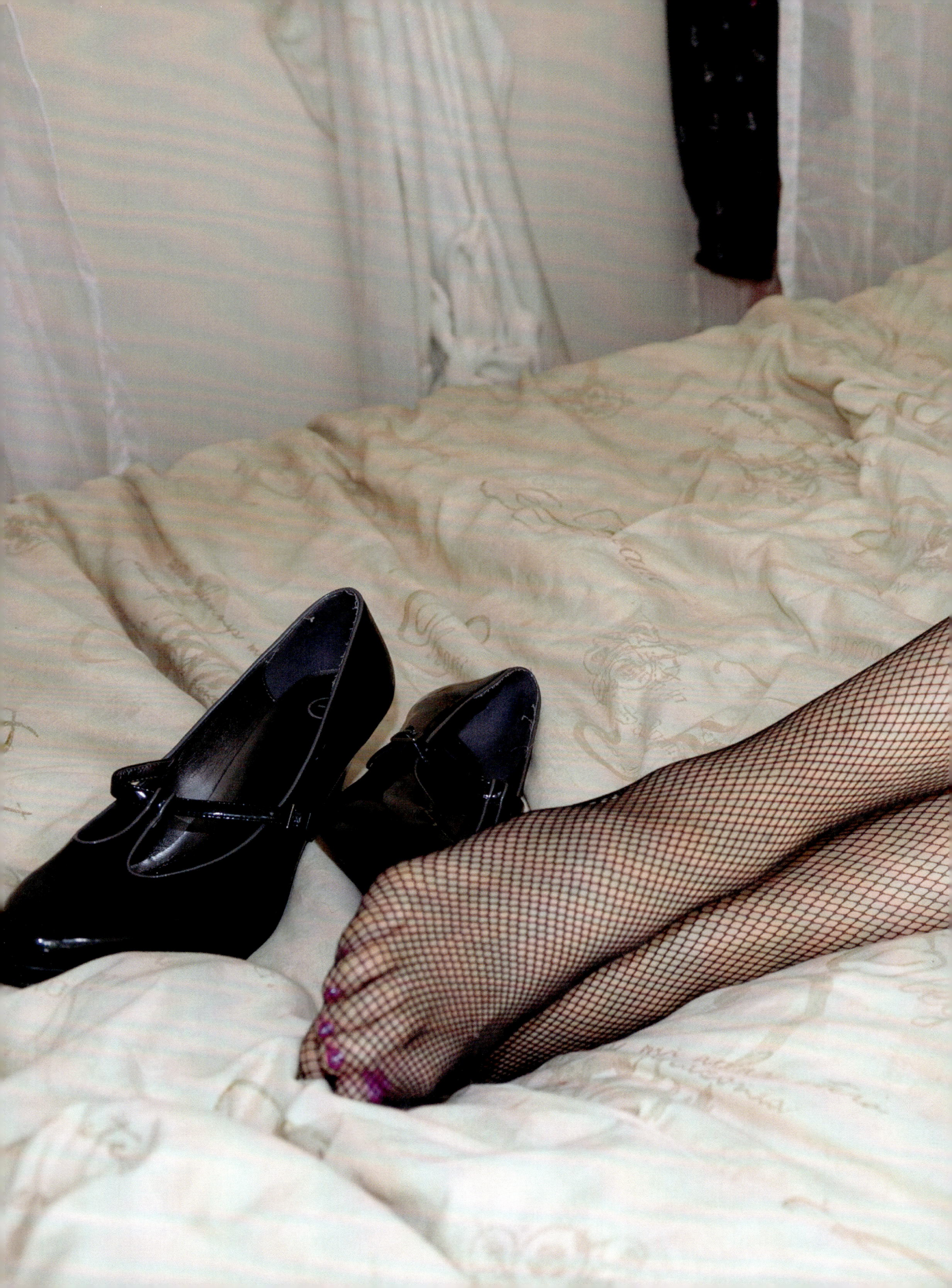

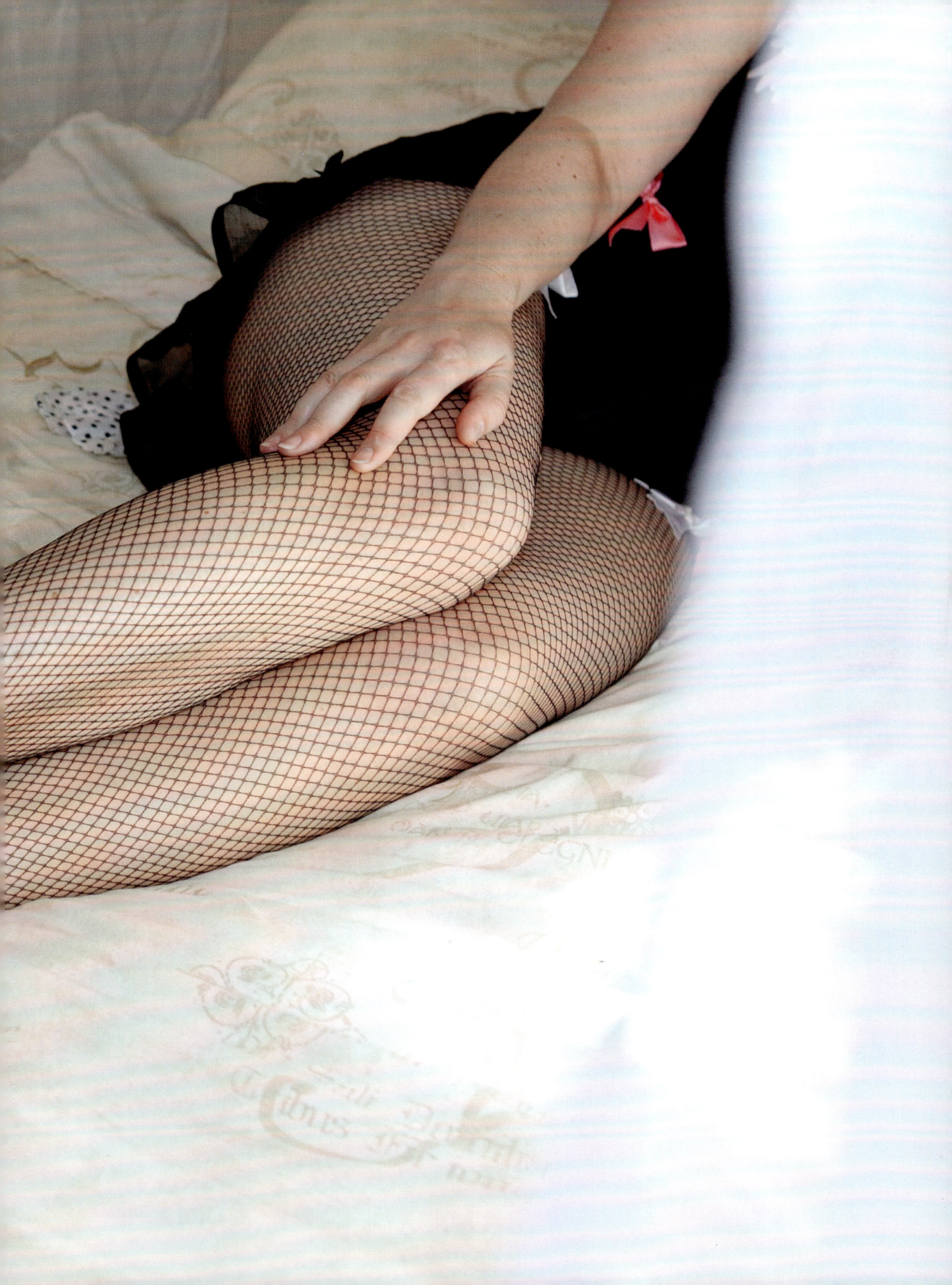

In Conversation with...

EMPRESS STAH

As a pioneer of adventurous burlesque cabaret, Empress's style of performance, formerly known as 'Twisted Cabaret' was popular in the 90s, sitting at the intersection of Neo-Burlesque, Circus & Live Art.

Prior to the burlesque renaissance, this act was relegated to a few club nights that were staging shows, predominantly via rave culture and where performers did circus acts alongside DJ music, in the style of a glorified podium dancer.

Empress explains she was the first to do this kind of act in the 90s:

'The Very Best of Empress Stah' was a self-produced show, staged at the Soho Revue Bar. I worked with the direct intention of bringing my cabaret acts out of the fetish clubs where I was performing and into the mainstream.'

ELENA GIBSON

For Elena, Burlesque performance is about being authentic, unashamedly joyful and open. It's about unapologetically taking up space in this platform through expressing sexuality, drama and femininity.

Joyfully abandoning traditional patriarchal expectations and societal norms, and fully embracing and harnessing female sexual energy, Elena is constantly inspired and empowered as a performer in the Burlesque community.

'It has been a great honour and privilege to be part of a group of performers who share their art, stories, wisdom and themselves as work in progress and are constantly evolving.

This job requires an incredible amount of erotic and emotional labour; a huge part of what we sell is energy as we create intimacy and bespoke connections whilst being completely in control of ourselves and our audience.'

HONEY MOON

For Honey, Burlesque was all about storytelling and incorporating drama from the past into the story of the present. Making the show as exaggerated and glamourous as possible in terms of music, costume and dance, Honey was inspired by fantasy, history and societal politics. She embraced layers within her costumes and characters, drawing on past heroines and dramas, and reworked these stories into her favourite shows. Honey has made lasting friendships within the Burlesque community.

'My Madame du Pompadour act is my favourite, the music used was Sweet Dreams (Marilyn Manson) and layer upon layer of costume. The top layer of the dress was made from a pattern dating from the 18th century.'

DOLLY ROCKET

With her 40 years in the showbiz industry, having hosted leading nights at clubs, including London's Café de Paris, Burlesque has played a central role in Dolly's life.

Working with many diverse and talented performers, she has loved seeing new acts at her weekly shows and celebrates Burlesque as a great avenue for both men and women's self-expression.

'I see performers from all kinds of backgrounds, both culturally and theatrically and some who just had the call and desire to follow their rhinestone hearts, as I did!

THERESE LA TEASE

Therese started out in the sunny seaside town of Eastbourne, in dance troupe Les Ooh La Las, performing high octane can-can in Sussex venues and at Glastonbury Fire & Dance stage.

Joining trailblazer Stella Starr and Vavavavoom, Therese found her feet as a burlesque and cabaret performer, featuring her solo routines for the London Burlesque Festival at legendary venues the Soho Revue Bar and Bush Green Hall, with her original can-can peel.

Therese joined cabaret and burlesque performer Baby Bones in Club Smooch and Trailer Trash at Brighton's original Komedia venue.

Alongside burlesque and cabaret performances, Therese took to the catwalk for Brighton Frocks with designer Chrissy Nicholson-Wild in Brighton, and Alternative London Fashion Week. Therese also worked with Stan Keetley, photographer in alternative location photoshoots.

In 2014, Therese decided to hang up her dance shoes and go behind the camera, photographing the shows she had been a part of, working with Betty Nails' Sassy Cabaret to capture the drama of live performance and worked on studio-styled promo photoshoots. She says, 'We were an amazing team working together tirelessly to produce high-quality shows.'

PANDORA FOX

After seeing a friend perform at an intimate Burlesque gig, Pandora was captivated by the joy, creativity and inclusivity of the Burlesque community and how the audience were enraptured.

Despite the personal turmoil of suffering from low self-esteem and body dysmorphia, with her mother being fatally ill at just 46 years old, Pandora decided to take up an opportunity to raise funds for a hospice with a stage performance and quickly discovered a deep determination and motivation inside herself.

She crafted a debut routine to a classic Doris Day melody and created every detail of her costume with care and precision. She joined a burlesque group and was mentored and supported, finding solace and comradery amongst a new community of friends.
'Stepping onto the stage for the first time in a vibrant Brighton theatre, adorned in my alter ego's glamour, my fears dissolved into the spotlight. Embracing the comedic aspect of performance, I discovered a newfound passion for crafting witty routines, rooted in self-deprecation and celebration of imperfections.

Balancing shows with my career became second nature, each performance a testament to self-acceptance and embracing individuality. Burlesque became a medium through which I challenged my own insecurities and fostered a profound appreciation for the human form. Through laughter and creativity, I not only entertained audiences but also embarked on a journey of personal growth.

Though my days on stage have ended due to career demands, the bonds forged, and memories made within the burlesque community remain cherished. Attending local shows, I just love the infectious energy backstage, reminiscing about rehearsals and ensuring our costumes were stage ready. Burlesque may no longer be my focus, but its spirit continues to inspire and bring joy to my life.'

HONOUR MISSION

Launching into her Burlesque career shortly after the death of her mother, Honour's journey was almost serendipitous. Inspired by a hairstyle change into a 50s roll and deep copper waves, she bumped into Stella Starr one evening, and was encouraged to join a troupe and quickly found herself performing onstage solo in full gingham and cowgirl style.

There followed prosecco-teapot meet-ups with other Burlesque performers and, after observations of her 6ft height, and with friends helping her produce the show, Honour embarked on her trademark act – 'Attack of the 50 ft Woman'. The performance ran internationally, and Honour was invited to showcase solo acts at Brighton's Club Smooch, went on to be part of award-winning shows and acts, and remains the figurehead at Brighton's March of the Mermaids.

'It was an era I won't forget; it was full of all the emotions and pure escapism. It was empowering and brought out the best most joyful nights. There is nothing like standing ovations to cheer the sadder days stricken with grief.'

STELLA STARR

Launching 'Vavavavoom! Burlesque' in 1997 and having directed and performed in Burlesque shows since the early 90s, Stella remembers that time of her life as a fabulous technicolour dreamscape filled with feathers, glitter and high jinks, both on stage and off.

This was also a time of political movement in Burlesque, raising awareness of inclusivity and accessibility, both onstage and in the audience. Stella went on to perform globally, until family and care commitments overtook her Burlesque career. Her last solo performance was with Tease-o-rama 2012 in San Francisco.

'I was driven by a political feminist stance on women reclaiming their sexuality and power.

I was fortunate to work with an incredible group of performers - including an extraordinary range of strong creative women.'

DEBBY BESFORD

My fascination surrounding female stage performers was born from my background as an artistic roller-skater. Creatively expressing myself to music, on skates at high speed, and incorporating jumps and spins was incredibly empowering and exciting. My teenage years as a performer gave me confidence and motivation to explore the world with curiosity and passion.

Years later as a documentary photographer, I became fascinated by the burlesque world. These performers are adventurous, skilful and courageous, proudly displaying their unique creativity and personality in their stage appearances.

Placing myself within this project felt liberating and playful. I feel doing this transposes the notion of the voyeur by putting myself in the observer's eye. I enjoyed the element of mystery and got a clear sense, momentarily, of what it feels like to be on the other side of the camera.

There is no order to the text or the photographs in this book. It is intended that the viewer spends time looking at the details of each interior, finding clues that only scratch the surface of the performer's identity.